THE
EARTH
JAMES TAYLOR

THE
EARTH
JAMES TAYLOR

ReadersMagnet, LLC

The Earth
Copyright © 2018 by James Taylor

Published in the United States of America
ISBN Paperback: 978-1-948864-77-0
ISBN Hardback: 978-1-948864-78-7
ISBN eBook: 978-1-948864-79-4

All rights reserved. No part of this publication may be reproduced, stored in a retrieval system or transmitted in any way by any means, electronic, mechanical, photocopy, recording or otherwise without the prior permission of the author except as provided by USA copyright law.

The opinions expressed by the author are not necessarily those of ReadersMagnet, LLC.

ReadersMagnet, LLC
10620 Treena Street, Suite 230 | San Diego, California, 92131 USA
1.619.354.2643 | www.readersmagnet.com

Book design copyright © 2018 by ReadersMagnet, LLC. All rights reserved.
Cover design by Ericka Walker
Interior design by Shemaryl Evans

ACKNOWLEDGMENTS

To my precious wife Loretha; who has stood by my side in my efforts and being fully supportive to me in this endeavor and to our children [young adults] James Jr and Tweetie.

To Apostle Cammy Mitchel and Mattie Mitchel of Holy Light Deliverant Church, Pastor and Assistant Pastor respectively. Thanks for your devotion in the truth of God, devoting yourselves to the Faith in which we stand.

To Elder and Pastor Eddie Seaverson: thanks for your devotion in your spiritual teachings of God's love, in which you have been a major influence in my life. I pray that God may bless you in all of your endeavors.

To Pastor Gloria Harp: thanks for your life long lesson of how Godly love is manifested in a human being. May you stand steadfast in the love and faith that you have in God and his people.

To my family that have known the ways of God and have prayed for me in my endeavors, may God bless every one of you; spiritually, physically and financially.

CONTENTS

Preface 9

Part 1: Noah's Descendants

Chapter 1: Color In The Sons Of Noah.................................... 13
Chapter 2: Shem's Semitic Lineage 15
Chapter 3: Ham And His Hamic Lineage................................ 24
Chapter 4: King Nimrod, Son Of Cush................................... 29
Chapter 5: Abraham 37
Chapter 6: Isaac 43
Chapter 7: Jacob 45
Chapter 8: Intermarriage And Intermixing
 In The Tribes Of Israel 50
Chapter 9: Ancient Egyptian Ethnicity.................................... 62
Chapter 10: Prophecy Of The Fate Of Israel 68

Part 2: God's Love And Guidance

Chapter 11: God's Truth (Love) 81
Chapter 12: Wisdom And Power 91
Chapter 13: A New Commandment.. 96
Chapter 14: Yahweh's Name Has Power 100
Chapter 15: Identifying The Truth.. 102
Chapter 16: Accepting Your Calling 117

Biography 129
Selected Bibliography And References 131
The Origin Of Man: God's Creation Of Color........................ 137
Index.. 139

PREFACE

This book is simply an effort of this Minister of the Gospel to reveal the truth. It is not written to offend or to characterize one race better than another. I present this work praying through the Holy Spirit that it will draw anyone who reads its contents. I pray that it will draw those who have rejected Christ and Christianity, perhaps because of questions and concerns related to race and Christian faith, to a commitment and faith in Lord Jesus Christ. I make no claims to being a scholar, theologian, anthropologist, historian, linguist or scientist: yet, I have labored diligently to be biblically-based, theologically true, anthropologically accurate, historically honest, etymologically enlightened and scientifically sound. I am a preacher of the gospel of the Lord Jesus Christ. Therefore, I make no apologies for preaching at certain points in this manuscript the biblical truth. This recorded truth is biblically sound and supported by historical records, including the biblical doctrine that has being preached for hundred of years. This doctrine which have been preached by hundred of thousands of American ministers have excluded some of the true Israelites. In saying this, it has robbed people of color from the hope and faith that the truth would have encouraged.

I am deeply indebted to all who have blazed this trail before me. I have sought to give credit to whom credit is due. The book reflects the toil and tears of numerous writers and speakers whose efficiency and eloquence have inspired and informed me. Some have been lost in memory and are quoted here without citation. Without their work, I would have been unable to provide answers to questions that have concern regarding many race and the Bible.

It is my desire that these pages inspire others to explore and ethnic factor in scripture, Christian history and contemporary society. If the truth has inspired you, I encourage you to share with others, that they too maybe inspired in the knowledge that has been hidden for so many years. This information is edifying, encouraging, inspiring and interesting to those of us who believe and are curious about the role of the Black Man recorded in biblical and historical Christianity.

The fact that people of color have played an extremely important role in biblical and classical Christianity recorded in biblical and historical Christianity has been a neglected factor in theological education. Our colleges and Seminary Training Centers have neglected their duties as a teacher of biblical information that was of profound importance, therefore weakening the potential ministers that attended these Training Centers and Institutions. This was the main reason I haven't attended any of these important and necessitated Spiritual Training Centers. Therefore being without this important training; I truly believe God words, "I will teach you all things", and therefore I dedicated myself to study to show myself approved, rightly dividing the words of truth. I pray that you find this work informative and edifying. I present this work in Christ's name and for his glory.

PART 1

Noah's Descendants

CHAPTER 1

COLOR IN THE SONS OF NOAH

When God created man and he was created perfect and no sin or blemish was found in him, after Man sinned (Adam and Eve), he lost his perfection and became evil. Yahweh/God decided to destroy man and He performed it by flooding the Earth. After the flood, Noah was the leader of an eight-adult members clan. In Abrahamic religions, **Noah** was the ***tenth and last*** of the antediluvian Patriarchs. The story of Noah and the Ark is told in the Genesis flood narrative. The Biblical account is followed by the story of the Curse of Ham. Outside Genesis his name is mentioned in 1 Chronicles, Isaiah, Ezekiel, the Gospels of Matthew and Luke, Hebrews and the 1st and 2nd Epistles of Peter. Man has sought a higher power as long as the 1st man (Adam) came to the garden. Man waxed evil in the sight of YAHWEH; therefore He destroyed mankind in the flood. Only eight people were left on the Earth after the flood water rescinded, Noah and his three sons, and their four wives were saved. Noah's three sons are named;

Japheth was the father of the Japhetic race, **Shem** was the father of the Semitic race and **Ham** was the father of the Hamic race. I will not list Japheth's sons and descendants in detail as I will Shem and Ham's descendants, because the emphasis of this book is only with the latter two sons.

In his five hundredth year Noah had three sons. In his six hundredth year God was saddened at the wickedness of mankind and He sent a great deluge to destroy all life, but because Noah was "righteous in his generation." God instructed him to build an ark and save a remnant of life. After the Flood, Noah offered a sacrifice to God, who promises never again to destroy all life on earth by flood and creates the rainbow as the sign of this "Everlasting covenant between God and every living creature of all flesh that is on the earth, also known as the Noahic covenant. After this, Noah became a husbandman and he planted a vineyard and he drank of the wine and became drunk and was uncovered within his tent. Noah's son Ham, the father of Canaan, saw the nakedness of his father and told his brethren and Noah cursed Ham's son Canaan. Some historians, scholars and theologians have erroneously stated "Noah cursed Ham, but that wasn't the truth. I will speak on the curse in more detail in chapter 4. Noah died 350 years after the flood at the age of 950, the last of the immensely long-lived antediluvian Patriarchs. The maximum human lifespan, as depicted by the bible diminishes rapidly thereafter from almost 1,000 years of life to the 120 years of Moses. Most people don't know the history of mankind. I contend that this history is important in our walk with God (YAHWEH). I will provide information that I have found in my research of the ***history of man*** after the flood that was somewhat shocking to me [things rumored, but wasn't biblically taught]. I had read numerous books, seen movies and pictures of the Noah and his descendants which lead me to be very skeptical in my initial research and of my findings. I will share with you the final results of my research that is supported by biblical and historical records.

CHAPTER 2

Shem's Semitic Lineage

Japheth was the father of the Gentiles nations Gen.10:5, In Gen. 10:2, Japheth is ascribed seven sons: Gomer, Magog, Tiras, Javan, Meshech, Tubal, and Madai. According to Josephus (Antiquities of the Jews I.6): Recorded history show these people lived in numerous areas including *Turkey* (Cappadocians) and additional areas; western most protrusion of *Asia*. 1 Chron. 1:7 'Rodanim,' the island of Rhodes, west of modern Turkey between Cyprus and the mainland of *Greece*. Madai is a son of Japheth and one of the 16 grandsons of Noah in the Book of Genesis of the Hebrew Bible. Biblical scholars have identified Madai with various nations from the Mitanni of early records and the Iranian Medes of much later records. The Medes, reckoned to be his offspring by Josephus and most subsequent writers, were also known as Madai, including in both Assyrian and Hebrew sources. The Kurds in Turkey still maintain traditions of descent from Madai. According to the Book of Jubilees (10:35-36), Madai had married a daughter of Shem and preferred to live among Shem's descendants, rather than dwell in Japheth's allotted inheritance beyond the Black Sea; so he begged his brothers-in-law, Elam, Asshur and Arphaxad until he finally received from them the land that was named after him,

Media. Another line in Jubilees (8:5) states that a daughter of Madai named **Melka** married Cainan, who is an ancestor of Abraham also mentioned in older versions of Genesis: (Cainan ancestor of Abraham. Cainan, the son of the Arpachshad is mentioned in most manuscripts of the Gospel of Luke 3:36). This reference to Cainan is present in the Septuagint and Samaritan versions of the Book of Genesis, as well as in the Book of Jubilees however, the early Christian apologists Irenaeus and Eusebius believed it to be an error, as do many modern interpreters, mainly on the basis of his **omission** from the Masoretic (Hebrew) version.

Shem was the son of Noah and the father of Arphaxad. Shem is noted to be one of three sons of Noah in the Hebrew Bible. He is most popularly regarded as the eldest son, though some traditions regard him as the second son. Genesis 10:21 refers to relative ages of Shem and his brother Japheth, but with sufficient ambiguity to have yielded different translations. The verse is translated in the KJV as "Unto Shem also, the father of **all** the children of **Eber**, the brother of Japheth the elder, even to him were children born.". However, the New American Standard Bible gives, "Also to Shem, the father of all the children of Eber, and the older brother of Japheth, children were born." Genesis 11:10 recalls Shem was still 100 years old at the birth of Arphaxad two years after the flood, making him barely 99 at the time the flood began; and that he lived for another 500 years after this, making his age at death 600 years.

Arphaxad was one of the five sons of **Shem** Genesis 10:22; 11:10. Seven generations followed Arphaxad before *Abraham*, while he lived till after the settlement of Abraham in the land of promise and the rescue of Lot from the four kings. He died A. M. 2096, aged four hundred and thirty-eight.

Other ancient Jewish sources, particularly the Book of Jubilees, point to Arpachshad as the immediate progenitor of Ura and Kesed, who allegedly founded the city of Ur Kesdim (Ur of the *Chaldees)* (See pages 8-11) on the west bank of the Euphrates (Jub. 9:4; 11:1-7)—the same bank where the city Ur is located. Arphaxad was born the year after the Deluge. He died at the age of 438 years (**Genesis 11:10-13; 1 Chronicles 1:17, 18; Luke 3:36**).

Elam was the son of Shem who spoke a language called Afroasiatic. The Afroasiatic language family was originally referred to as "**Ham**ito-Semitic", a term introduced in the 1860s by the German scholar Karl Richard Lepsius. The name was later popularized by Friedrich Müller in his Grundriss der Sprachwissenschaft (Wien 1876-88). In lieu of "Hamito-Semitic", the Russian linguist Igor Diakonoff later suggested the term "Afrasian", meaning "**half-African,** half-Asiatic", in reference to the geographic distribution of the phylum's constituent languages. Early American definition of an Afro-American is one that ancestors came from the continent of Africa. But scholars and historians have narrowed Africa's original boundaries, which ancients maps includes major parts of Asia.

Aram was the son of Shem who lived according to the Book of Jubilees (9:5,6) in all of the land between the Tigris and Euphrates rivers to the north of the Chaldees to the border of the mountains of Asshur and the land of 'Arara (Ancient relics indicates Black Heads lived in this area). The Arameans appear to have displaced the earlier Semitic Amorite populations of ancient Syria during the period from 1200 BC to 900 BC, which was a dark age for the entire Near East, *North Africa*, Caucasus, Mediterranean and Balkan regions, with great upheavals and mass movements of people. There was some **synthesis** with neo **Hittite** populations in northern Syria and south central Anatolia and a number of small Syro-Hittite states arose in the region, such as Tabal. Hittites are listed in Book of Genesis as second of the twelve Canaanite nations that descended from **Heth**. In 332 BC. the region was conquered by the Greek ruler, **Alexander the Great**. In *323 BC* this area became part of the Greek Seleucid Empire, at which point Greek replaced Aramaic as the official language of Empire. 1st to 3rd Centuries AD and the Aramaic language gradually supplanted Canaanite in Phonecia and Hebrew in Israel/Palestine. The 1st century historian Flavius Josephus, among many others, recounted the tradition that these five sons of Shem were the progenitors of the nations of Elam,

Assyria, Chaldea, Lydia, and **Syria**, respectively. Semitic is still a commonly used term for the Semitic languages, as a subset of the **Afro**-Asiatic languages denoting the common linguistic heritage of **Arabic, Aramaic, Akkadian, Ethiopic, Hebrew** and **Phoenician** [all having black nations] languages.

Lud was another son of Shem. Some scholars have associated the biblical Lud with the Lubdu of Assyrian sources, who inhabited certain parts of western Media and Atropatene. Muslim historian Muhammad ibn Jarir al-Tabari (c. 915) recounts Lud was the progenitor of not only the Persians, but also the **mixed** Amalekites and Canaanites and all the peoples of the East, Oman, Hejaz, Syria, Egypt, and Bahrein. We know that Canaan and Miziriam are progenitors of the Canaanites and the Egyptians, respectively. All offsprings of Noah's three sons intermixed and married within the entire family of Noah.

Sala was the son of *Arpachshad,* (the King James Version) is an ancestor of the Israelites according to the Table of Nations in Genesis 10. He is thus one of the table's "seventy names". He is called **Shelah** in 1 Chronicles 1:18 and **Sala** Septuagint and Luke 3:35. In the ancestral line from Noah to Abraham, he is the son of Arpachshad (in the Masoretic Text) or Cainan (in the Septuagint) and the father of Eber. The name "Eber" for his son is the original eponym of the Hebrew people, from the root *'abar,* "to cross over". Salah's age at death is given as 433 (Masoretic) or 460 (Septuagint).

Eber was the son of Sala is an ancestor of the Israelites, according to the "Table of Nations" in **Genesis 10-11and 1 Chronicles 1**. Genesis 10:21 "Unto Shem also, the *father* of all the children of Eber." This give all of Eber sons birthrights to larger allotted land area by being considered sons of Shem. In Jewish tradition, Eber, the great-grandson of Shem, refused to help with the building of the Tower of Babel, so his language was not confused when it was abandoned. He and his family alone retained the original human language, Hebrew a language named after Eber (Heber), also called lingua humana in Latin. Gen.10:30 "And their dwelling was from Mesha, as thou go unto Sephar a Mount of the east". Ancient

Mesha was located near the Red Sea, very close and some argue it was in King Nimrod, the Cushite kingdom. The Book of Jubilees mentions the name of "Nebrod" (the Greek form of Nimrod) only as being the father of **Azurad**, who was the wife of Eber and the mother of Peleg and Joktan (8:7). Peleg was born when Eber was 34 years old. Eber: Peleg and Joktan are the only two sons mentioned in the bible that were born to Eber, but their mother Azurad is not mentioned.

Some scholars think the biblical statement "The Earth was divided" mean the continents were divided and began to shift. I believe the land was divided into inheritance rights or possibly this was the time discussed in Genesis 11 when the people of the earth were divided linguistically at the Tower of Babel. The name Peleg means divided. Peleg and his people lived in a city named after Cush, the son of Ham, father of Nimrod "**Kish** of the *Chaldeans.*" There is an excavated palace of Sargon I [Nimrod] of Agade, a native of Kish and a great temple built by Nebuchadnezzar and Nabonidus in the later Babylonian period. The site also yielded a complete sequence of *pottery* from the Sumerian period to that of Nebuchadnezzar. Peleg and his brother Joktan people lived in the land of the "**Sabaeans**" and Cush's clans and sub-clans lived in these same areas (See Joktan and Peleg, grandsons of Nimrod and their relations to Abraham in Chapter 5). In light of current exposed history, Peleg and Joktan descendants were of the same ethnicity as Ham descendants.

Joktan was the second son of Eber, and father of Almodad, Sheleph, Hazarmaveth, Jerah, Hadoram, Uzal, Diklah, Obal, Abimael, **Sheba**, Ophir, Havilah and Jobab. Jobab is identified by some scholars as the man **"Job"** from the book of Job in the Bible. The King James 1611 version bible genealogy chart lists Job as a descendant of Abraham and Keturah; she was a Cushite. Biblical scholars, archaeologists and others have tried to determine the exact location of **Ophir** [Land or city named after Ophir, son of Joktan].

Vasco da Gama's companion Tomé Lopes reasoned that Ophir would have been the ancient name for Great Zimbabwe in

Zimbabwe, the main center of sub-African trade in gold in the Renaissance period—though the ruins at Great Zimbabwe are now dated to the medieval era, long after Solomon is said to have lived. The identification of Ophir with Sofala in Mozambique was mentioned by Milton in *Paradise Lost* (11:399-401), among many other works of literature and science. Most modern scholars still place Ophir either on the coast of either Pakistan or India, in what is now Poovar, or somewhere in **southwest Arabia** in the region of modern Yemen. This is also the assumed location of Sheba [brother of Ophir]. All of these scholars' beliefs indicate Ophir, son of Joktan, as well as the land or city of Ophir major population were ethnic people.

Job 30:30 states, "My skin grows **black** and peels; my body burns with fever". There are no known disease(s) that cause Caucasians' skin of their entire body to turn black. Blacks' skin have **many shades**, therefore Job was saying, "My skin is getting darker." Every race's skin gets darker by the heat of the sun, but only ethnic people say "My skin is getting darker or blacker."

In Pseudo-Philo's account (ca. 70), this prince (Joktan) command all persons to bake bricks for the Tower of Babel; however, twelve, including several of Joktan's own sons, as well as Abraham and Lot, refuse the orders. Joktan smuggles them out of Shinar and into the mountains, to the annoyance of the other two prince. The traditional history of the Ethiopian Orthodox Church also maintains that Joktan's sons would take no part in the tower building, and that they were thus allowed to preserve the original Ge'ez language—which their descendants, the Agazyan (Ethiopian), carried across the Red Sea into Ethiopia as they **mixed** with the Cushitic and Agaw people to form the hybrid Habesha race. *(*Conflict of Adam and Eve): All the kings who reigned over that country were called Sabaeans. The Sabaeans or Sabeans were an ancient people speaking an Old South Arabian language who lived in what is today **Yemen**, in the south west of the Arabian Peninsula. Some scholars suggest a link between the Sabaeans and the Biblical land of Sheba (See Joktan II, son of Abraham and his son Sheba was living in a land called the land of Sabeans, in which Eber and Peleg had previously lived). Joktan's name is preserved in the modern tribal federation called Kahtan or Qahtan located in present day **Saudi Arabia,** whose descendants lived in Paliga on the Euphrates, just above the mouth of the Khabur River.

Ur Kaśdim or Ur of the Chaldees is a biblical city mentioned in the Book of Genesis that refers to a location where the Patriarch Abraham lived. In 1927 Leonard Woolley identified Ur Kaśdim with the Sumerian city of Ur in southern Mesopotamia, where the Chaldeans had settled around the 9th century BCE; Ur lay on the boundary of the region called Kaldu (Chaldea, corresponding to Hebrew Kaśdim) in the first millennium BCE. 1915 International Standard Bible Encyclopedia article *"Ur of the Chaldees"*, understood this as an identification of Uruk (biblical **Erech**, the city that King Nimrod built) with Ur Kaśdim and this supports other proof in this book that Ur of Chaldees was an ethnic city.

The identification with Ur Kaśdim accords with the view that Abraham's ancestors may have been moon-worshippers, an idea based on the possibility that the name of Abraham's father Terah is related to the Hebrew root for moon (y-r-$ḥ$). The Book of Joshua says "Joshua said to all the people, "This is what the Lord, the God of Israel says, 'Long ago your ancestors, including Terah the father of Abraham and Nahor lived beyond the Euphrates River and *worshiped other gods.*'"(Joshua 24:2). Scholars say Serug was the first of the patriarchal line to abandon monotheism and turn to idol worship, teaching sorcery to his son Nahor. The book "Conflict of Adam and Eve" notes: "And in those days Ragu [Reu] was 180 years old and in his 140th year Yanuf [Apophis] reigned over the **land of Egypt.**" This was a god-like king and I believe he was demonic spiritually, therefore Reu started worshopping Apophis and these two individuals were kinsmen (See 1611 King James version bible genealogy chart listing ancient Caldeans Kings directly under Ham and the first recorded king was Nimrod, son of Cush).

Reu or Ragau in Genesis was the son of Peleg and the father of Serug, thus being Abraham's great-great-grandfather. He was 32 when Serug was born and lived to the age of 239 (Genesis 11:20, according to the Masoretic text. The Book of Jubilees named his mother as Lomna of Shinar **(see Genesis 10:28)**, and his wife as Ora, daughter of Ur Kesed. Those people of *Shinar* were of Ham's ethnicity. Nimrod was the Emperor in this area, later in Abraham life King Amraphel rule this land, both Emperiors were descendants of Ham (Father of the Black race). **Genesis 14:1-7.**

Serug was the **son** of *Reu* and the father of *Nahor*, according to Genesis 11:20-23, was the great-grandfather of *Abraham*. In the Masoretic text that modern Bibles are based on, he was 30 when Nahor was born, and lived another 200 years, making his age at death 230. The Septuagint (LXX) and Samaritan Pentateuch texts state that he was 130 on fathering Nahor, and the Samaritan gives his age at death as 230, stating he lived another 100 years, while the LXX has 200, making him 330 at his death. He is called *Saruch* in the Greek version of **Luke 3:35**. Further details are provided in Book of Jubilees, where it gives the names of his mother, Ora (11:1), and wife Milcah (11:6). It also states that his original name was Seroh, but that it was changed to Serug in the time when Noah's children began to fight wars, and the city of **Ur Kesdim** was built, where Serug lived.

Nahor in the bible refer to more than one person in the Hebrew Bible. Two biblical people are descendants of Shem and one is noted as the "Father of Terah." In Genesis Chapter 11, Nahor, son of Serug was born and raised in the Sumerian city of *Ur* on the Euphrates River of lower *Mesopotamia*, about four Millenia ago. Nahor's wife; *Ijose,* is only mentioned in Jubilees 11:8 as the daughter of Nesteg, both were from the Chaldees, and this means both were ethnic. Nahor lived to be 148 years old and his son Terah was born to him at the age of 29. He was also the *grandfather* of Abraham, Nahor II and Haran were both descendants of Shem. Consider where the Canaanites and Cushite lived [Most of Ham descendants lived in the same land as Shem descendants] and you will see the norm of life of intermixing and intermarrying. **Terah** lived 70 years and begot Abram [Abraham], Nahor and Haran.

Terah was a wicked idolatrous priest who manufactured idols. In Jewish tradition, Abram is considered to be the eldest of three sons who was opposed to his father's idol shop.

After Abram smashed his father's idols and chased customers away, Terah brought his unruly son **before King Nimrod**, who threw him into a fiery furnace, yet Abram miraculously escaped. The Zohar says that God saved Abram from the furnace. Terah and Abraham came from the city of **Ur** of the **Chaldeans.** Genesis 10:10 says that the "**beginning** of his **kingdom** was Babel, Uruk, Akkad and Calneh in the land of Shinar" (Mesopotamia). Ham's descendants intermixed among Shem's people and support the idea that "dark" colored people were living as Chaldeans and extra-tribal marriages occurred often. There are numerous different religious positions on this issue and I will support mines with traceable proof. The sons of Shem and Ham were the Sumerians. Livingston suggests that Sumerian Kish "Ancient Days", the first city established in Mesopotamia after the Flood, took its name from the man known in the Bible as *Cush,* son of Ham [Father of the black race]. There is biblical history of Ham's descendants [Zuazims] and denotes a once-mentioned town where Chedorlaomer defeated the **Zuzim** in the war of four against five kings **(Genesis 14:5).** When Abram had an encounter with God, he directed his family to leave their native land and go to the land of Canaan. Terah, their father coordinated the gathering of his family to journey west to their destination. They followed the Euphrates River with their herds to the Padan-Aram region. This was about halfway along the Fertile Crescent between Mesopotamia and the Mediterranean, in what is now southeastern *Turkey.*

CHAPTER 3

Ham and His Hamic Lineage

*H*am was the son of Noah and his name means ("hot" or "burnt"), according to the Table of Nations in the Book of Genesis, was a son of **Noah** and the father of **Cush, Mizraim, Phut** and **Canaan**. He was the youngest son of Noah (Genesis 9:24). Mizraim and Canaan descendants are sons of Ham, thereby the name Ham is sometimes used to indicate Egypt (**Ps 105:23**) "The land of Ham". (See pictures on the internet revealing ancient Kings' tombs with detailed paintings showing Ancient Egyptians were ethnic people and King James 1611 bible genealogies chart). For the meaning of this name Ham, Jones' Dictionary of Old Testament proper names confidently renders Heat, **Black** and as some scholar attested "Goes off on the tried and commonly rejected ramble that connects heat with blackness and then with sin." Jones rather reluctantly admits that Ham was the grandfather of the world's **first Emperor Nimrod,** but quickly relativizes this feat by fantastically stating, 'no doubt [Ham] was the sole introducer of the *worship of the sun*' and thundering, even while the hand of God was bearing him up in safety in the ark of gopher wood, the leaven of his horrid idolatry was working in his breast."

Genesis 5:32 notes Noah begat Shem, Ham and Japheth while he was still 500 years old. (Noah was 600 years old at the time of

✦ THE EARTH ✦

the flood in Genesis 7.) The story of Ham is related in Genesis 9:20-27. According to the Bible, Ham was one of the sons of Noah who moved southwest (modern compass direction) into Africa and parts of adjoining areas of Asia and was the forefather of the nations there. The Bible refers to the land of Egypt as "**the land of Ham**" in Psalms 78:51; 105:23,27; 106:22; 1Ch 4:40.

Some modern scholars view the *curse of Canaan* in Genesis 9:20-27 as an early Hebrew rationalization for Israel's conquest of Canaan. When Noah cursed Canaan in Genesis 9:25, he used the expression "Cursed be Canaan; a servant of servants. He shall be to his brethren" NKJV. The expression "servant of servants", otherwise translated "**slave of slaves**", NIV emphasizes the extreme degree of servitude that Canaan will experience in relation to his "brothers". In the subsequent passage, "of Shem . . . may Canaan be his servant, the narrator is foreshadowing Israel's conquest of the promised land. Biblical scholar Philip R. Davies explains that the author of this narrative used Noah to curse Canaan in order to provide *justification* for the later Israelites driving out and enslaving the Canaanites.

Cush was the son of Ham. Cush (also Kush) was according to the Bible, the eldest son of Ham, brother of Mizraim, Put and Canaan and the father of the Biblical characters **Nimrod** and Raamah, mentioned in the "Table of Nations" in the Genesis 10:6 and I Chronicles 1:8. He is traditionally considered the eponymous ancestor of the people of Cush, dark-skinned people inhabiting the country surrounded by the River Gihon, identified in antiquity with Arabia Felix (i.e. **Yemen**) and Aethiopia (i.e. all Sub-Saharan Africa, particularly the Upper Nile). Aethiopia first appeared as a geographical term in classical sources, in reference to the Upper Nile region, as well as all the regions south of the Sahara desert.

The Greek historian Herodotus specifically used it to describe all of Sub-Saharan Africa. The name also features in Greek mythology, where it is sometimes associated with a kingdom said to be seated at Joppa or elsewhere in **Asia**. Cush's sons were Seba, Havilah, Sabtah, Raamah and Sabtechah and Raamah sons: Sheba,

Dedan **Gen. 10:7.** The ancient relics of the ancient Egyptians prove they were Black. Cush descendants additionally were dwelling in and around the Euphrates and lived in his son; King Nimrod's kingdom that included Babylon, Erech, Accad, and Calneh in Shinar Babylonia.

Mizraim, the son of Ham, his name represents the **land of Egypt** with the dual suffix—āyim, perhaps referring to the "Two Egypts": Upper Egypt and Lower Egypt. Egypt was known by the names Musuru, Musru, Misir or Masri in other languages, and Mizraim is probably simply a phonetic transliteration into Hebrew of any of them. Mizraim's sons were Ludim, Anamim, Lehabim, Naphtuhim, Pathrusim, Casluhim (out of whom came Philistim/**Philistines**) and Caphtorim. According to George Syncellus, the *Book of Sothis*, supposedly by Manetho, had identified Mizraim with the legendary first pharaoh **Menes**, said to have unified the Old Kingdom and built Memphis. Recents discovers refutes Mizraim and Menes was the same Leader or King. According to Genesis 10:6, Mizraim (a son of Ham) was the younger brother of Cush and elder brother of Phut and Canaan, whose families together made up the Hamite branch of Noah's descendants. King James 1611 Bible genealogical chart list Egyptians as the Descendants of Mizraim, the son of Ham; Father of the black race.

Phut or **Put** is the third son of Ham in the biblical Table of Nations **(Genesis 10:6; cf. 1 Chronicles 1:8)**. Put (or Phut) is associated with Ancient **Libya** by many early writers. Josephus writes: "Phut also was the founder of Libya and called the inhabitants Phutites (Phoutes), from himself: there is also a river in the country of Moors which bears that name; whence it is that we may see the greatest part of the Grecian historiographers mention that river and the adjoining country by the appellation of Phut (Phoute): but the name it has now has been by change given it from one of the sons of Mezraim, who was called **Lybyos**." (AotJ Book 1:6/2). Pliny the Elder Nat. Hist. 5.1 and Ptolemy Geog. iv.1.3, both place the river Phuth on the west side of Mauretania (modern Morocco). Ptolemy also mentions a city Putea in Libya (iv.3.39).

✦ The Earth ✦

Canaan, according to the King James 1611 Version of the bible was a son of Ham and grandson of Noah and the father of the **Canaanites**. He was the recipient of the so-called "Curse of Ham". Genesis 10 (verses 15-19), Canaan was the ancestor of the tribes who originally occupied the ancient Land of Canaan: all the territory from Sidon (named after his son Sidon) or Hamath in the north to Gaza in the southwest and Lasha in the southeast. This territory is roughly the areas of modern day Israel, Palestine, Lebanon, western Jordan, and western Syria. These people were "dark" skinned [descendants of Ham] and did not live in Africa. Canaan's firstborn son was Sidon, who shares his name with the Phoenician city of Sidon in present-day Lebanon. His second son was **Heth**. Canaan's descendants, according to the Bible, include: Sidonians, i.e. the **Phoenicians**, **Hittites**, children of Heth, **Jebusites**, **Amorites**, Girgashites, **Hivites**, Arkites, Sinites, Arvadites, Zemarites, Hamathites.

The highlighted clans intermixed with Shem descendants on numerous occasions in the Bible. The German historian Johannes Aventinus (fl. c. 1525.) writes: "According to traditional Ethiopian histories, Canaan's son Arwadi and his wife Entela crossed **from Asia** into Ethiopia in 2101 BC and the Qemant tribe were said to be descended from their son, **Anayer**. There is further an Ethiopian tradition that two other Canaanite tribes, viz. the Sinites and Zemarites and they also entered Ethiopia at the time it was ruled by the Kingdom of Kush [Nimord] (See city of Kish). They became the Shanqella and Weyto peoples, respectively. The Persian historian Muhammad ibn Jarir al-Tabari (c. 915) recounted a tradition that the wife of Canaan was named Arsal, a daughter of Batawil son of Tiras and that she bore him the "Blacks, Nubians, Fezzan, Zanj, Zaghawah and all the peoples of the Sudan". According to archaeologist Jonathan N. Tubb, "Ammonites, Moabites, Israelites and Phoenicians undoubtedly achieved their own cultural identities and yet ethnically they were all Canaanites', the same people who settled in farming villages in the region in the 8th millennium BC.

In chapter 8 "Intermarriages and intermixing in the Tribes of Israel", the descendants of Ham's sub-clans; including those listed by regional names on page 11-12, married the descendants of Shem's [Semitic] clans and intermixed their genes into **all** the tribes of Israel (especially into the **Levi, Simeon** and the tribe of **Judah**). This fact have been hidden for many years and will finally be revealed in detail, name by name, tribe by tribe or clan by clan, including sub-clans in this book. Scholars, Historians and Theologians have avoided this truth that has caused the lost of an entire ethnic group true history. This revelation of the TURTH is intended to encourage and not to condemn. "All things works to the good of those that loves the Lord" **Romans 8:28**

In King James 1611 version of the Bible genealogy chart of Ham, the **Caldeans** are listed as descendants of of Nimrod. King Amraphel, who was one of Ham's descendants fought in The War of Kings. Historians and Scholars have used ambiguous terms to cloud the true ethnicity of these biblical forefathers. These people were called Sabeans and Black Heads and mixed creating people of color [ethnic], thereby creating a colorful world. The names of these forefathers, their clans and tribes are clear indicators of the truth [ethnicity] that I will reveal in this book. This book does not only identify the ethnicity of these forefathers, but also to reveal the corrective acts God have in place toward the prideful and sinful nature of mankind. Thereby, this book is one of inclusiveness of all people, not exclusion of any group of people. All of mankind evolved from one man [Adam], making *all* mankind kinsmen. American definition of a black man is "One that came from the Continent of Africa" and these scholars overlooked the sons of ancient Canaan territory. All of the ancient Canaanite land was in **Asia**, not Africa and was the land of just one of Ham's sons. The Bible tells us that all Canaanites were not totally driven out of their land, the remaining lived among Israel and noted in the Book of Joshua, even in the city of Jerusalem, which the Canaanites called Salem. Most of the ancients rulers in biblical land area were descendants of Ham. According to the MATSYA PURANA, an ancient book from India, the world belonged to the **Kushites** [Cushites] or **Saka** (as they are sometimes called) for 7000 years.

CHAPTER 4

King Nimrod, Son of Cush

The cities and civilization in Nimrod's Kindom:

Babylon was the capital of the ancient land of Babylonia in southern Mesopotamia. It was situated on the Euphrates River about 50 miles south of modern Baghdad, just north of what is now a modern Iraqi town of al-Hillah. This land included Arphaxad, son of Shem descendants. The founders of the first Mesopotamian civilization were Sumerians. Mesopotamia was the Biblical land of Shinar (Sumer). The Sumerians left no doubt to how they viewed themselves racially. The Sumerians called themselves sag-gig-ga, "the **Black headed people.**" Sumer [ancient Kish] was at the crossroads of Asia, Africa and Europe. While Sumer was not a homogenous society, the Blackheads of Sumer were politically and socially dominant. (Introduction to the Study of African Classical Civilizations by Runoko Rashidi, London: Karnak House, 1992, pg. 69).

Sumer was the earliest ancient civilization of west **Asia.** Sumer was the foundation of the later civilizations of Babylonia and Chaldea. Nimrod was King and later widen his domain. The bible states, "He was a mightly hunter" (Spiritual Powers).

The Sumerian civilization, which ruled the southern portion of the fertile Tigris/Euphrates River Valley, sprang up around 3000 B.C. and lasted until about 1750 B.C. The Sumerians are often describes as "non-Semtic, pre-Semtic or non-Indo-European." The Scholars attempt to veil the fact that the Sumerians were black or ethnic people have been successful for many years. Historians and Theologians are willing to use any ambiguous term to cloud the true racial origins of the Sumerians. The name Nahrima in the Amarna letters denoted the region of the Upper Euphrates and its tributaries. Both Josephus and the Septuagint translate the name as Mesopotamia.

John Baldwin wrote: "The early colonists of Babylonia were of the same race as the inhabitants of the Upper Nile." (PreHistoric Nations by John D. Baldwin, New York: Harper & Brothers, 1869. H.G. Wells said that the "Sumerians appear to have been a *brownish* people with *prominent noses*." (A Short History of the World by H.G. Wells, New York: MacMillan, 1922, pg. 75) Sir Arthur Keith said that the Sumerians were dolichocephalic. (Mohenjo-Daro and the *Indus* Civilization: Being an Official Account of Archeological Excavations at Mohenjo-Daro carried out by the Government of *India* Between the Years 1922 and 1927 by John W. Marshall, New Delhi: Asian Educational Services, 1996, pg. 109) Dolichocephalism is a skull characteristic predominately found in Blacks. Based on the statuaries and steles of Babylonia, the Sumerians were "**dark** complexion (chocolate colour), short stature, but of sturdy frame, oval face, stout nose, straight hair, full head; they typically resembled the Dravidians, not only in cranium, but almost in all the details" (A Study in Hindu Social Polity by Chandra Chakaberty, Delhi: Mittal Publications, 1987, pg. 33).

Rudolph Windsor emphatically stated: "There is definitely a blood relationship between the Dravidian tribes of **India** and the Ethiopian Sumerians." (From Babylon to Timbuktu by Rudolph R. Windsor. Atlanta: Windsor's Golden Series, 2203, pg. 17). There were so many Black people in ancient Asia that Herbert Wendt wrote: "All indications point to the fact that **Asia** was the *cradle* of the black race." (It Began in Babel by Herbert Wendt. New York: Delta Dell Publishing Company, 1964, pg. 368.) The Black people of Egypt certainly influenced the Sumerians. The seeds of civilization in Sumeria passed through Egypt. Albert Churchward said that the Sumerians, Chaldeans and Babylonians obtained all their laws and learning from the Egyptians. (Signs & Symbols of Primordial Man by Albert Churchward, Brooklyn:A&B Books Publishers, 1993, pg. 209) Thereby, we can trace the roots of the Sumerian society back to black people. Nimrod, and later the Egyptians worshipped Sun gods. Exodus 7:9-12 recalls: "So Moses and Aaron went to Pharaoh and did just as the LORD commanded. Aaron threw his staff down in front of Pharaoh and his officials, and it became a **snake**."

Pharaoh then summoned wise men and sorcerers, and the Egyptians magicians did the same things by their secret arts: Each one threw down his staff and it became a snake. But Aaron's staff swallowed up their staffs. The main similarities of these two nations were that they worshipped an invisible God and made blood sacrifices. The Hebrew worshipped Yahweh and He has mighty Power. The Egyptians had numerous gods, which had power, but nothing like Yahweh. He is *almighty* and said it, "No god *is like me*, no other!" **Isaiah 44:6-8.** Those Egyptians really were worshipping demons. "For great is the Lord and most worthy of praise; he is to be feared above all gods" (Psalm 96:4). We worship an invisible God today, and Yahweh [Elohim] is the true and only God; the rest of the gods, once were Yahweh's Angles that were expelled from Heaven. Their leader [Lucifer] wanted to be like Yahweh Isaiah 14:14. "I will exalt my throne above the stars [Angels] of God, and I will sit also upon the mount [Yahweh's Throne] of the congregation" Isaiah 14:13. "**I will be like the Most High**" Isaiah 14:14. Yahweh wouldn't have it and kick him out of Heaven. "You shall be brought down to hell, to the sides of the pit" Isaiah 14:15. The Egyptians sorcerers' power source came from Lucifer and was on display during this event.

This next event show Yahweh's anger and power: Lev 10:1 And Nadab and Abihu, the sons of Aaron, took either of them his censer and put fire therein, and put incense thereon, and **offered strange fire** before the LORD, which he commanded them not. Lev 17:11-12: Aaron shall bring the bullock of the sin offering, which is for himself, and shall make an atonement for himself, and for his house, and shall kill the bullock of the sin offering, which is for himself. Aaron sons incorrectly performed this spiritual ritual. (v11) And he shall take a censer full of burning coals of fire from off the altar before the Lord, and his hands full of sweet incense beaten small, and bring it within the veil. This is what happened for Aaron's son's disobedience: So fire came out from the presence of the LORD and **consumed** them, and they died before the LORD. Jesus performed this Spiritual Ritual of Blood Sacrifice once, and finalized it on earth for all mankind by dying on the cross, rising from the dead, and ascending into heaven entering into the Holy of Holies, and shed his blood on the Mercy Seat (Blood Sacrifice) **Hebrews 10:9-23**.

I write this book to reveal the truth and to encourage any race that you can be Yahweh's chosen people and it not about how one look, financial status, religious Preference, but only about your individual relationship with your Creator. I'm not an intellectual, scholar or historian, I am an unknown minister of the New Covenant/testament doctrine. I want you to know about all of ways of Yahweh, including what happens when you are lifted up in pride. Proverbs 16:18. **"There is no man that is good**, no not one" Rom 3:8

These were the cities of the Cushites:

Erech: According to the Book of Genesis Erech was an ancient city in the land of Shinar, the second city built by king Nimrod. While earlier scholars such as Jerome (4th century) had identified Erech with the Syrian city of Edessa (now within Turkey), the modern consensus is that it refers to the Sumerian city-state of **Uruk**, in south Mesopotamia. I will continue to show all of the Middle East and who were the ancient inhabitants.

✦ The Earth ✦

Calneh was one of the four cities founded by Nimrod, according to the Book of Genesis in the Bible. **(Genesis 10:10).** Its identity is uncertain and remains a mystery. The verse in question reads; "The beginning of his kingdom was Babl, and Erech, and Accad, and Calneh, in the land of Shinar." W.F. Albright proposed that this is not actually a proper name, but merely the Hebrew word meaning "all of them". Calneh ("Chalanne") was identified with Ctesiphon in Jerome's Hebrew questions on Genesis, ca. 390 CE. Easton's 1897 Bible Dictionary silently follows Sir Henry Rawlinson in interpreting the Talmudic passage Joma 10a identifying Calneh with the modern Nippur, a lofty mound of earth and rubbish situated in the marshes on the east bank of the Euphrates, but 30 miles distant from its present course, and about 60 miles south-south-east from Babylon.

Calneh is also mentioned in the Book of Amos in the Bible and some have also associated this place with Calno which is mentioned in similar terms in the Book of Isaiah **Amos 6:2, Isaiah 10:9.** This is identified by some archaeological scholars as Kulnia, Kullani or Kullanhu, modern Kullan-Köy, between Carchemish on the Euphrates River and Arpad near Aleppo in **Northern Syria**, about ten kilometers southeast from Arpad. Canneh, which is mentioned in the Book of Ezekiel 27:23 as one of the towns with which **Tyre** carried on trade was associated with Calneh by A.T. Olmstead in his book "History of **Assyria**." Xenophon mentioned a Kainai on the west bank of the Tigris below the Upper Zab. The Tigris River (/ˈtaɪgrɪs/) is the eastern member of the two great rivers that define Mesopotamia, the other being the Euphrates. The river flows south from the mountains of southeastern **Turkey** through **Iraq**. Calneh figures among the conquests of Shalmaneser III (858 BCE) and Tiglath-Pileser III.

The **Akkadian Empire** was an empire centered in the city of Akkad [Accad] and its surrounding region in ancient Mesopotamia which united all the indigenous Akkadian speaking Semites and the Sumerian speakers under one rule [Nimrod]. Ethiopia boarders were larger than they are presently today. Ancient Ethiopia included largely Assyria and possibly all of **Yemen**. They were relatives of King Nimrod, and this blood relation is confirmed by his daughter Azurad marriage to Eber.

During the 3rd millennium BC, there developed a very intimate cultural symbiosis between the Sumerians and the Semitic Akkadians, which included widespread bilingualism. Akkadian gradually replaced Sumerian as a spoken language somewhere around the turn of the 3rd and the 2nd millennium BC (the exact dating being a matter of debate). Nimrod was the son of Cush and he also built Babylon in which had two elements in the city population in the beginning Genesis 10:10. The finds of recent explorations in the Mesopotamian valley reveal that these ancient inhabitants were **Black** with the cranial formation of **Ethiopians**.

Shinar is a biblical geographical locale of uncertain boundaries in Mesopotamia. The name may be a corruption of Hebrew Shene neharot ("two rivers"), Hebrew Shene arim ("two cities") or Akkadian Sumeru from the Sumerians' name for Sumer, which meant perhaps "land of the civilized lords" or "native land". Though belonging to the same Semitic ethnic group, they are to be differentiated from the Aramean stock and the Assyrian king Sennacherib, for example, is careful in his inscriptions to distinguish them. When they came to possess the whole of southern Mesopotamia, the name "Chaldean" became synonymous with "Babylonian", particularly to the Greeks and Jews. In the Hebrew Bible, Abraham is stated to have originally been from "Ur of the Chaldees" (Ur Kasdim). If this city is to be identified with the Sumerian Ur, it would be within the original Chaldean homeland south of the Euphrates, although Chaldeans were not extant in Mesopotamia at the time of Abraham. According to the Book of Jubilees, Ur Kasdim and Chaldea took their name from Ura and Kesed, descendants of Arpachshad, son of Shem. Blacks have been told we came only from Africa and that is not the truth. In modern geography the name Ethiopia is confined to the country known as Abyssinia, an extensive territory in East Africa. In ancient times Ethiopia extended over vast domains in both

Africa and Asia." This area is the home of all of Ham and Shem descendants territory (See where the Bible states these clans lived).

"It seems certain," declares Sir E. A. Wallis Budge, "that classical historians and geographers called the whole region from India to Egypt, both countries inclusive, by the name of Ethiopia, and in consequence they regarded all the dark-skinned and Black people who inhabited it as **Ethiopians**. In addition Budge notes that, "Homer and Herodotus call all the peoples Ethiopians that live in **Sudan, Egypt, Arabia, Palestine** and Western **Asia** and **India**." (Ibid., p. 2.) Herodotus wrote in his celebrated history that both the Western Ethiopians, who lived in Africa, and the Eastern Ethiopians who dwelled in India, were black in complexion, but that the Africans had curly hair, while the Indians were straight-haired. The aboriginal Black inhabitants of India are generally referred to as the Dravidians, of whom more will be said as we proceed.

Another classical historian who wrote about the Ethiopians was Strabo, from whom I quote the following: "I assert that the ancient Greeks, in the same way as they classed all the northern nations with which they were familiar as Scythians, etc., so, I affirm, they designated as Ethiopia the whole of the southern countries toward the ocean." Strabo adds that "If the moderns have confined the appellation Ethiopians to those only who dwell near Egypt, this must **not be allowed to interfere** with the meaning of the ancients."

The Semitic [Shem-Jews] family can also trace their origins from this area in north-eastern **Africa**. "Kasdim," "land of Kasdim" or "the Chaldeans," is the usual designation in the Old Testament for the land and the people in Jeremiah 50:10, Jeremiah 51:24, Jeremiah 24:5 and Jeremiah 25:12 (See names of clans and cities on pg 6-8). Jeremiah clearly states **intermixing** of **all** these tribes or nations that were living in this area with the Hebrews had occurred Jeremiah 25:20 "And all of the **mingled** people". The corresponding Greek form with l for s follows the Assyr-Bab Kaldu, mat Kaldi, Chaldean, land of the Chaldeans. Kasdim is possibly connected with the name of Kesed (Kesedh), nephew of Abraham (Genesis 22:22) and may be derived from the Assyr-Bab root kasadu, "to capture." It suggest that the Chaldeans were originally tribes of nomadic plunderers (compare Job 1:17). Isn't that claim presently made today? This was the land Nimrod [Cushite] ruled (See Towel of Babal). Most of the cities mentioned in the Genesis chapter 10 were built by Nimrod and none of his cities the bible states he built were in Africa, but mostly in Asia.

Some Scholars and I believe that Asshur in Genesis 10:11 was the son of Nimrod from the daughter of Shem's son Asshur. The Hebrew tribal name and marriage pattern supports this view. Nimrod wife is believed to be Raama, daugther of Asshur, who was the son of Shem. They had a son and named him Asshur after his grandfather. Verse 11 in Genesis 10 states, "**Out of that land** [Nimrod's] went forth Asshur and built Nineveh." This view is supported by the bible stating Asshur built Nineveh in **only** Ham's biblically recorded account and **not** in Shem and his sons biblical family account and allotted lands. I will continue to show this customary marriage and name pattern in this book. Ham and his sons are listed in Gen. 10:6-20 and Shem and his sons start at Gen. 10:21, in which mentions only the name Asshur, but nothing is mentioned about him building a city. Other theologians believe Asshur, the son of Shem built Nineveh, but may not be of Nimrod's **race**. That theory is not possible considering Shem and Ham were brothers and one Asshur was Ham's great-grandson and the other Shem's son. Consider these men had 400-500 years life span. Noah had sons at age 500 years old and lived possibly up to 600 to 700, decreasing in the life time of his father Lamech's 777 years of life. The life span of these men after Noah continued to slowly decrease.

CHAPTER 5

Abraham

A**braham** is the founding father of the Israelites with a prominent role in Judaism and Christianity. The biblical story **(Gen 14:5)** of Chedorlaomer defeating the Zuzims in war also reveals the Power of Yahweh and His love for His people. Abraham had an army that totaled only 318 defeated possibly thousands of the Kings' soldiers. Those defeated kings had took Lot (Abraham nephew) when they defeated Sodom, Gomorrah, Admah, Aeboinim and Zoar (Gen. 14). Verse 17 states, "His [Abraham] return from the slaughter of Chedorlaomer and of the kings that were with him." Yahweh hand was mighty with Abraham. He took 318 men and went and destroyed Chedorlaomer and the other kings, including their armies and brought back Lot, who had been captured by them. Who can be against God's anointed?

Greece mythology mentions Thermopylae was held for three days against a vast Persian army by just 300 Spartans, 299 of which perished. Abraham battle actually happened, as well as Gibeon's 300 in the bible, but the Greek story; "The 300" is one in which historians terms as a "Myth". The story of Abraham is told in chapters 11:26-25:18 of the book of Genesis. It is essentially the history of the establishment of the covenant between Abraham and God. God calls Abraham to leave his land with his family and household in Mesopotamia in return for a new land, family and inheritance in Canaan, which was the promise land. Threats to the covenant arose (difficulties in producing an heir, the threat of bondage in Egypt and the lack of fear of God); but all are overcome and the covenant was established. America's Black slaves ancestors were Hebrews and I make this connection Abraham had married to two confirmed Black wives, Hagar; the Egyptian and Keturah; the Jebusite, also called Cushite after Cush, son of Ham.

The Book of Jubilees notes the name "Nebrod" (the Greek form of Nimrod) only as being the father of **Azurad**, the wife of **Eber** and mother of **Peleg** (8:7). This account would make "Nebrod" an ancestor of Abraham and hence of all Hebrews. Eber and his wife had another son name "Joktan". "After Peleg, Eber lived 430 years and begat sons and daughters" **Gen.11:17**. Joktan could have been borned many years after Peleg, his older brother. Jokan was the father of Keturah, Abraham's wife. Jotkan was possibly born anytime during the 430 years of his father life after the birth of Peleg. The verse in Genesis 10:25 notes "Peleg; in his days the land was divided." Joktan and his other brothers were allotted their share of Shem sons' allotted land, which was an equal share with their father Eber and his brothers inherited land. Genesis 10:21 "Unto Shem also, **the father** of **all** the children of Eber." Like wise, Joktan, Keturah's son ruled in the entire allotted land of his Grandfather Joktan, who had inherited land as one of the sons of Shem Genesis 10:21, This same allotted land latter was inherited by Joktan; the son of Abraham. In 2010 an ancient discovery was made in Nigerian of a Jebusite kingdom. The Jebusites ruled in Jerusalem in the time of David and the city was called Salem during Melchi*zedek* reign ("tzedek", meaning '**righteous**' (ness)' or 'justice') Genesis 14:8-9.

The location of this tribal discovery might surprise some because of it location [**Africa**]. The **Jebusites**, some were biblically known as *Canaanites*, but they were Cushite and Canaanite mixed and kin to the biblical clans of Sheba, the son of Raamah. Joktan, the son Abraham and Keturah also named his son Sheba to honor Sheba, the son of Raamah, who was the son of Cush, who was the son of Ham, who is historically know as the father of the **Black race**. (Genesis 10:7). There is an additional Cushite lineage with the Jebusites though Nimrod's daughter **Azurad**. The Jebusites had two main divisions: the Nago-Jebu and the Ketu-Jebu. Both divisions take the serpent as their totem. Ketu and Naga are two ancient words for serpent. In ancient Egyptian literature the cosmic serpent is called RahuKetu. Mizriam was the father of the Egyptians and the brother of Cush. Genesis contains a good deal of information on the Ketu-Jebu division, this division resided in Palestine and Arabia. Abraham paid tribute to the Ketu-Jebu priest Melchizedek (Salem/Jerusalem). Abraham's wife Keturah was of this division of Ketu and is evidenced by her name **Ketu-rah**. (Ancient names had meanings and Yahweh changes his servants name on numerous occasions according to their acts and accomplishments). Keturah resided at Beer-Sheba, which took its name from the first Sheba, who had a 500-600 years life span and he controlled the well there. The ancient word Beer means well. Abraham's wife after Sarah died was Ketu-rah and one of her sons was Joktan, the progenitor of the Joktanite **clans of Arabia**. All of Abraham's sons ruled in Joktan's land that was allotted to him, and Keturah bore six sons. The 1st Sheba was the 1st cousin of Azurad; daughter of Nimrod, who was Peleg and Joktan mother. The Semitic lineage is inherited though Peleg and his brother Joktan had his blessings also. It appears from historical records that part of Joktan inheritance was in Nigeria at the confluence of the Niger and Benue rivers which in the time of Abraham's ancestors were very great rivers.

No one should be surprised to find Jebusites in Nigeria, considering Cain and Enoch are associated with Nok on the Jos Plateau of Nigeria and Noah is associated with Bor-No in northern Nigeria near Lake Chad. Nevertheless the Joktanites would become a powerful presence in the Sinai and by their skills and generosity would enable the Israelites to come out of Egypt and survive in the wilderness. Some of the descendants of Joktan and Sheba hold an annual autumn feast at an oasis in the wilderness to celebrate the date harvest. This is the one time of the year that women and men may dance together. The date palm ("tamar") is a symbol of prosperity and fertility. The 'Id el-Tamar is a festival when the unmarried check out the pool of available matches. As is the custom from time immemorial, wife selection takes place at a well or an oasis. This name Tamar is again recorded in the bible as Daughter-in-Law of Judah, and mother of his twin sons; Perez and Zerah. Tamar [bore two sons from Judah] was a descendant of Joktan; the brother of Peleg and his daughter Keturah, who was the wife of Abraham Gen 11:19. I believe the Book of Jasher is incorrect with verse 45:23 stating, "And in those days Judah went to the house of Shem and took Tamar the daughter of Elam, the son of Shem, for a wife for **his first born Er**." Elam was described as "**Half-African**" by the Russian linguist Igor Diakonoff. Elam's daughter would have been hundreds of years older than Judah, when he looked for a wife for his son. Elam's first born bother Arphaxad lived 438 years and Elam's daughter would have lived less than her father and his brothers in longevity. Thereby, this recorded theory has no merits. This is why I believe the noncanonical was omitted from consideration of being added to the canonical bible.

I only use the book of Jasher for historical records, not as the bible that is factual. Abraham was nearly one hundred years old when Isacc was born, who was the grandfather of Er. After Er's death, Tamar waited for the youngest brother to become grown enough to marry him. The book of Jasher states, "Tamar was the daughter of Elam", this would be inconsistent with the age factor of Elam having a daughter young enough to marry Judah's sons Genesis 38.

A Jebu ruler-apparent ascended to the throne after he married a second wife." This explains Abraham's urgency to fetch a cousin bride for Isaac before his death. Following the marriage pattern of the rulers of his people, Isaac already would have had a *half-sister* wife in Beer**sheba** who is not mentioned in the bible.

In Pseudo-Philo's account (ca. 70), the first man named *Joktan* was **first** made prince over the children of Shem, just as Nimrod and Phenech were princes over the children of Ham and Japheth, respectively. Joktan II became prince over his grandfather's kingdom. This is possibly why the bible says "Abraham gave his sons gifts and sent them away from Issac", they already had a land inheritance though their brother Joktan. I believe according to Genesis 10:21 "Unto Shem also, the father of **all** Eber's children (land inheritance rights), Joktan became the 1st Prince of Shem. Joktan II, who was Abraham's son later became a prince after his grandfather Joktan, which is witnessed by his name and the customary pattern of being name after his relative. The traditional history of the Ethiopian Orthodox Church also maintains that Joktan's sons would take no part in the tower building and that they were thus allowed to preserve the original Ge'ez language—which their descendants, the **Agazyan**, carried across the Red Sea into Ethiopia as they mixed with the Cushitic (blacks) and Agaw people to form the *hybrid* Habesha race. This discovery proves the writers assumptions about Semitic Blacks are incorrect, they came not only from Ethiopa, but from all parts Asia. Keturah bore Abraham six sons, Zimran, Joktan, Medan, Midian, Ishbak, and Shuah, (**Genesis 25:1,2**). Keturah son **Midian** records note; four centuries later Moses flees from Egypt to the land of Midian, supporting Moses's first wife Zipporah was Midian's descendant. This also conveys Moses' father-in-law (Reuel/Jethro), which was a Priest of a different faith and later converted to be Yahweh's Priest. This conversion is reflected by Moses' actions toward his brother-in-law.

"Moses said to Hobab, the son of Reuel the Midianite; who was Moses' father-in-law, "We are setting out for the place about which the LORD said, I will give it to you. Come with us and we will treat you well, for the Lord has promised good things to Israel." We have learned over the years though ancient artifacts that Queen Sheba was a **black** woman. She ruled from Ethiopia and parts of Assyria/Arabia and Yemen. Her ancient relics prove she was of the Negroid race. "The queen of Sheba" (1 Kings 10:1-2; 1, Kings 10:10) ruled in Arabia and Ethiopia. She came (a distance of nearly a thousand miles) from the uttermost parts of the earth," as then known, to hear the Wisdom of Solomon (**Matthew 12:42; Luke 11:31**). Four principal Arab people are named the Sabeans; Atramitae or Hadramaut, Katabeni or Kahtan or **Joktan**, and the Mimaei. Sheba was a town in **Simeon's** allotted land (Joshua 19:2), (See Chapter 15; the sons of Simeon); one was possibly the Shema in Joshua 15:26. The name Sheba comes from Ham's grandson "Sheba."

The kingdom of Sheba is referred to in Yemeni and Ethiopian history, both are considered mixed Cushites. The Septuagint uniformly translates Cush as Αιθιοπία "*Aithiopia.*"

Jeremaih 35: 3 "Then I took Jaazaniah the son of Jeremiah, the son of Habaziniah, and his brethren, and all his sons, and the **whole house** of the Rechabites" [descendant of Midians]. The Midianites were a large Kingdom and their rule have been proven and they were black people [Cushites].

Jeremiah 35:18-19 Jeremiah blessed the Rechabites [descendants of Midian, son of Abraham], "You have obeyed Jonadab your father, and **kept all his percepts**, and done according unto **all** that he had **commanded** you." Jonadab percepts were the Commandments of Yahweh. Number 25:10-15 reveals to us by the Midianite woman action that was pleasing God is it not about skin color; rather it's about one's relationship and actions to Yahweh's Commandments.

Judges 4:17-24 speaks of Jael the wife of **Heber**; the Kenite [descendant of Midian]; Moses' brother-in-law.

Some historians and scholars have stated "Blacks have never ruled a civilized nation", which was not true. All the nations surrounding present day Israel was ruled by Canaanites. Ancient Egypt was ruled by Blacks.

Melchizedek ruled Salem, which was the first Jerusalem and located in Canaanites territory, and Abraham honored him by paying him tithes.

Nimrod, the Cushite King possibly was the first Emperor.

Later in this book, I will reveal the truth about the Hebrew Kings ethnicity.

CHAPTER 6

Isaac

*I*SAAC; the son of Abraham and Sarah is described in the Hebrew Bible as the father of Jacob and Esau. Isaac was one of the three patriarchs of the Israelites. According to the Book of Genesis, Abraham was 100 years old when Isaac was born and Sarah was beyond childbearing years. Isaac was the only biblical patriarch whose name was not changed, and the only one who did not leave Canaan. When Isaac was 40, Abraham sent Eliezer, his steward into Mesopotamia to find a wife for Isaac from his nephew Bethuel, whose family also had a **cushite origin** (Eber's wife Azurad). Eliezer chose Rebekah for Isaac to marry. After many years of marriage to Isaac, Rebekah had still not given birth to a child and was believed to be barren. Isaac prayed for her and she conceived. Rebekah gave birth to twin boys, Esau and Jacob. At the age of 75, Isaac moved to Beer-lahai-roi after his father died. When the land experienced famine, he removed to the Philistine land of Gerar where his father once lived. This land was still under the control of King Abimelech (Cushite) as it was in the days of Abraham. Like his father, Isaac also deceived Abimelech about his wife and also got into the well business.

He went back to all of the wells that his father dug and saw that they were all stopped up with earth. The Philistines did this after Abraham died. So, Isaac unearthed them and began to dig for more wells all the way to **Beersheba**, where he made a pact with Abimelech, a pact just like in the day of his father. Isaac favored Esau and Rebekah favored Jacob. Isaac grew old and became blind. He called his son Esau and directed him to procure some venison for him in order to receive Isaac's blessing. While Esau was hunting, Jacob after listening to his mother's advice, deceived his blind father by misrepresenting himself as Esau and thereby obtained his father's blessing. Thereby, Jacob became Isaac's primary heir and Esau was left in an inferior position.

According to Genesis 25:29-34, Esau had subsequently sold his birthright to Jacob for "bread and *a* stew of lentils." Thereafter, Jacob was sent into Mesopotamia (Cushite) to take a wife of his own family. After 20 years working for his uncle Laban, Jacob returned home. He reconciled with his twin brother Esau, then he and Esau buried their father, Isaac, in Hebron at the age of 180. Shem was still living when Isaac was born. Genesis 11:11, "And Shem lived after he begot Arphax' an additional 500 years and begot sons and daughters." The years from the birth of Arphaxad to the birth of Issac were about 485 years and outlived Terah, Abraham's father. Shem out lived eight generation of sons.

CHAPTER 7

Jacob

Jacob was the son of Isaac, and he left his father's house because of the hostility between him and his brother Esau; because he received the blessing of the first born instead of his older brother (previously sold to him for food). Gen. 29:10 Notes; "Laban was Jacob mother's brother." The Book of Jasher 45:5 states; "**Adinah (1)** was the wife of Laban and mother of Leah and Rachel. Laban and Adinah were descendants of Azurad, the Cushite and the wife of Eber. Only Ham and Shem descendants lived in this massive area of land. The Book of Jubliees 34:20 notes Simeon, the son of Jacob, wife was Adlba'ap; the **Canaanite** [black woman]. God changed Jacob's name to Israel. Additionally, I believe Simeon's wife name was changed due to a Godly favored act she performed. Judah was another one of Jacob's sons, which had a son named Er, son of a Canaanite *[black]* woman, named **Shuah**. She bore Er, which died, and she bore another son named Onan, who Yahweh killed for being evil. Their 3rd son was named *Shelah*. Shelah had the only clansmen left among Judah and Shuah first three sons and he was born at Chezib. In the biblical text after Yahweh killed Shelah's two older brothers, (Er and Onan), Judah was unwilling to allow Tamar to marry the younger brother. Judah concern was that Tamar might have been cursed and Shelah might die if he married her, so Judah told her to wait until Shelah had grown up. When Shelah grew of age, Judah neglected to marry him to Tamar. In the Book of Chronicles. **Shelah** is identified as the having a **clan** containing a subclan named **Er**, which was most likely named to honor his deceased eldest brother. Shuah's black genes were transferred into her descendants' blood line and *mixed* again into the Hebrew tribes that were already somewhat Black or an ethnic race. ". *(*See Chapter 15*)*—Jacob/Israel had *black genes* from both sides of his *family* [father and mother].

The sons of Shelah; who was the son of Judah were:
1. **Er**, the father of Lecah.
2. **Laadah**, the father of Mareshah, and the families of the house of the linen workers of the house of Ashbea.
3. **Jokim**, the men of Chozeba (potters that worked for the King).
4. **Joash** has no historical records
5. **Saraph**, who ruled in Moab-meaning they were Ruth's kinmen *(Shelah's mixed*-Moab-ites*)*.
6. **Jashubi-Lehem** has no historical records.

The later result of this cursed incident was that Tamar gave birth to twin boys from Judah, her father-in-law and named them, **Perez** and Zerah (who were twins). The entire story is found in Genesis chapter 38. The Cushites ethnicity in **Perez** was through his mother Tamar and father Judah, which was transferred to **Ruth** and **Boaz**.

Jesus lineage is recorded though Perez [Pharez], the son of Judah. See Matt: 1 and this verse proves black genes was in the tribe of Judah.

Jasher 45:1 ***Reuben*** had married Eliuram; who was a **Canaanite** [black] and she bore him Memuel, Yamin, Ohad, Jachin and

Zochar, a total of five sons. Reuben had more sons; which is noted in 1 Chon 5:3. "The sons of Reuben, the oldest son of Israel, were Hanoch, Pallu, Hezron and Carmi." 43,730 Reubenites under the age of twenty upon leaving Egypt entered the Promise Land Num. 26:7). 1 Chon 5:4-9. The biblical first person named **Hanoch** was named in line to his ancestors Enoch; grandfather of Noah or maybe to Enoch; son of Cain, and likewise his cousin Hanoch received the same name; who was the son of Midian; the son of Abraham. Beerah was a leader of the Reubenites when they crossed into the promise land. The two Hanochs were relatives, the other descendants are listed according to their genealogical records: Jeiel the chief, Zechariah and Bela son of Azaz, the son of Shema (named afther his ancestor; Shem), the son of Joel. They settled in the area from Aroer to Nebo and Baal Meon. To the east they occupied the land up to the edge of the desert that extends to the Euphrates River, because their livestock had increased in Gilead. Fifty-two descendants of the inhabitants of Nebo returned from exile with Zerubbabel (Ezra 2:29 Nehemiah 7:33). The place was in the land of Judah and is named after Bethel and Ai. There is nothing, however to guide us as to its exact position. It may be represented by either Belt Nuba, 12 miles Northwest of Jerusalem or Nuba, which lies about 4 miles South-Southeast of 'Id el-Ma' (Adullam). Considering their history of intermixing, I contend the name "Nuba" alone speaks of the race of people that lived in the Nubians territory of Africa; who were **very dark-skinned** people". This is possibly why Jeremiah stated, "Can an Ethiopian change his skin?" Jer. 13:23 This verse wasn't a confirmation that the ancient Hebrew wasn't Black or ethnic, as some have scholars attest, but the Israelites skin were lighter in completions than the Ethiopians [Nubians]. But in Jeremiah 14:2 he described the tribe of Judah **skin color**, "They are **black** unto the ground." This verse is also supported by the ethnicity of Judah's wives.

Simeon was the son of Jacob and Leah, he was father of the Israelites and the father of the tribe of Simeon. Although some classical rabbinical sources argue that the mother of his children and his wife was **Bonah,** one of the women from Shechem of the **Canaanites,** he also had an additional wife named **Adinah**; who may have been renamed Bonah. Jasher 28:28 states "**Adinah** daughter of **Job**" (See Job 30:30; which stated "My skin is ***black***") and his daughter was Simeon's wife. The King James Bible in **Job 42:14** name Job daughters; Jemima, Kezia and Keren-happuch. We know biblical names were changed by their acts or events that the people experienced (e.g. Abram to Abraham and Jacob to Israel). Simeon had a son named Shaul and some scholars and historians confuse him as Israel 1st King, who was also named Saul, but King Saul was a Benjamite.

Jasher 45:21 **Benjamin** went afterward and took another wife; **Aribath,** the daughter of **Shomron**; who was the son of Abraham by Keturah; the Cushite. Jasher 45:22 states, "**Aribath** bore unto Benjamin, Achi, Vosh, Mupim, Chupim and Ord. King Saul father was named Kish, as in the Chaldean city of Kish, which was named after Cush, son of Ham; historically known as the father of the Black race. The Benjamites were ethnic people and descendents of Peleg, who was son of Eber and **Azurad.**

Jasher 45:7 **Aphlaleth**: Wife of **Dan,** daughter of Chamudan; the **Moabite**. The Moabite language is an extinct Canaanite language. Many comparisons of Biblical Hebrew with the language of the Mêša inscription appear in Wilhelm Gesenius' Hebrew grammar.

Jasher 45:13-17 **Adon,** wife of **Asher,** daughter of Aphlal, who was son of Hadad; who was the son of **Ishmael;** who was Abraham's son from the Egyptian named Hagar.

Hadurah was the second wife of Asher; sister of Adon, Hadurah conceived and bore unto him Yimnah, Yishvah, Yishvi and Beriah, a total of four sons. The Lord gave her Wisdom and Understanding (Spiritual Gifts). These Gifts are noted in **1 Cor. 12.**

Jasher 45:19 And **Zebulun** went to Midian and took for a wife **Merishah** the daughter of Molad; who was the son of Abida, who was the son of Midian and brought her to the land of Canaan. **Midian** was the son of Abraham and Keturah; the Cushite.

Testaments of the 12 Patriarchs: "**Aena:** Daughter of **Rotheus**; who was the mother of Zilpah and Bilah", they were the handmaidens of Rachel and Leach; the wives of Jacob, and Zilpah and Bilah were his concubines.

Naphtali1: "And Rotheus was of the **family of Abraham**, a Chaldean, feared God, and was free-born and **noble**. He was taken captive and was bought by **Laban**, and he was given a wife named Aena. She was Laban's handmaid, and she bore a daughter and called her **Zilpah**, after the name of the village in which he had been taken captive. Next she bore **Bilhah**, saying, my daughter is eager after what is new, for immediately she was born eager for the breast. Zilpah was Leah's handmaid, and she bore **Gad** and **Asher** to Jacob. Bilhad was Rachel's handmaid, and she bore **Dan** and **Naphtali** to Jacob.

According to The Book of Jasher, **Issachar** married *Aridah*, the younger daughter of Jobab; the son of Joktan; who was the son of Abraham and Keturah. The Torah states that Issachar had four sons, who were born in Canaan and migrated with him to Egypt. Iasschar's sons potential wives were from their mixed Cushite families that entered Egypt or from the Egyptian women, who were descendants of Mizraim; the son of Ham; father of the **Black race**.

The Book of Jubilees is considered canonical by the Ethiopian Orthodox Church as well as Jews in Ethiopia, where it is known as the Book of Division (Ge'ez: *Mets'hafe Kufale*). I will use both; The Book of Jasher and The Book of Jubilees, which are westernly known as noncanonical books only as historical records. I will use the Bible as proof to support intermixing and marriages between the descendants of Ham and Shem occurred numerous times, so many times these ancient Hebrews definitely were ethnic people.

CHAPTER 8

INTERMARRIAGE AND INTERMIXING IN THE TRIBES OF ISRAEL

The Book of Ruth is a book of the Hebrew Bible/Old Testament. In the Jewish canon it is included in the third division or the Writings (Ketuvim). In the Christian bible, it is treated as a history book and placed between Judges and 1 Samuel. It is named after its central figure; Ruth the **Moabitess**, the great-grandmother of King David. According to the Gospel of Matthew, Ruth was an ancestress of Jesus. I contend that Jesus had Black ethnicity in his earthly genes. The Book of Revelations in the Bible notes; "Feet like bronze and **hair like wool**." Look around today, there are many shades of skin color in black in America, as well as in other parts of the world that Blacks lived. Some Blacks are so light-skinned that their skin looked like bronze in color. Distinctive features of a large flat nose, or **woolly hair**, large lips are clear indicators of our black ethnicity. Remember, "one drop of black blood" was the rule as justification for slavery, but Yahweh doesn't see color that way. Yahweh possibly thought, "To encourage you, I see how people will feel about your race; I'll send my son to earth with your features." There isn't anything in black ethnicity that makes blackness less or better than any other race of people. Biblically, it about God's grace and love to all mankind and the multiple colors he created in them. God takes the lowly of things and make it acceptable and loved, if only to Himself. Yahweh states, "I'll be with you and in you, if, and only if, You **hear** my voice and follow me". Ruth was called a Moabitess and her in-laws were Ephrathites (tribe of Joseph's half Egyptian son). According to the Old Testament (e.g., Genesis 19:30-38), the Moabites belonged to the same ethnic stock as the Israelites and were descendant of Moab; son of Lot. Lot was the nephew of Abraham.

I will list this historical information in detailed order to make it is easier to trace the Hebrew families' names and clans that point unmistakably to people of color [blacks]. Salmon is the son of Nahshon; who was married to Rehab of Jericho (the **Hittite**, who was from a large clan from **Heth; the Canaanite**). Rehab bore Boaz, Ruth's husband. Salmon, Rahab's husband is mentioned in 1 Chronicles 2:10-11, Ruth 4:20,21, and Matthew 1:4. Ruth and Boaz son was named Obed, who was the father of Jesse and he was father of **King David**. Boaz is mentioned in both the Gospel of Matthew and the Gospel of Luke as an ancestor of Jesus, **'according to the flesh'**. Some Scholar argue that Jesus' lineage from David was though his non-biological father Joseph, but that is not the truth. *Mary*, who was Jesus' mother also had a blood line from King David and it is recorded in Luke 3:23-38. Joseph was clearly the son of Jacob Matthew 1:16, so this verse in Luke 3:23 states "Son of Heli" somewhat conflicts with the Matthew account. Luke's verse should be understood to mean **"Son-in-Law** of Heli." Boaz father was named Salmon, and Salmon's father was Nahson. Nahson and his sister had a direct link to another Hebrew tribe (I talk about this connection later in this chapter). Salmon was from a Clan mixed with the Canaanites and he married Rahab of Jericho; the Hitite, by whom they bore Boaz. This is Salmon's family tree; **Judah**-Perez-Hezron-Ram-Amminadab-Nahshon-**Salmon**-Boaz-Obed-Jesse-King David. Solomon; who was the son of King David and recorded in 1 Chronicles 3:10-11, Ruth 4:20,21, and Matthew 1:4 with a lineage to Jesus.

1 Chononicles 2 continues the customary uncle-cousin marriage and name pattern, proving the Cushite and mixed Canaanite gene was still being pass down on both sides of those Hebrew marriages. **Salmon** broke the marriage custom and married Rahab, a descendant of Heth, by whom he had Boaz. Rahab was a *harlot* [prostitute; whore] and Yahweh made her bloodline part of his son Jesus. **Nahshon** was according to the Book of Exodus, the son of *Amminadab*; descendant in the fifth generation of **Judah** and he was the brother-in-law of Aaron and was an important figure in the Hebrew's passage of the Red Sea. According to the Jewish Midrash he initiated by walking in head deep until the sea split. "Walking by faith and not by sight" 2 Corinthians 5:7 Amminadab's wife had to be kin to him or she was Egyptian. Aaron's sons (Priests and workers of the Temple) were kinsmen to all the descendants of Judah's tribe by Nahshon's sister. Their ancestors were Judah and Tamar descendants, and they also were descendants of Azurad, the wife of Eber and mother of Peleg and Joktan. Nahshon did not survive the forty-year sojourn in the wilderness to enter the Promised Land. Nahshon was appointed by Moses as God commanded to be prince and military commander of the Tribe of Judah (Numbers 2:3; 10:14). His tribe was fourth in the order of the Patriarchs, yet at the dedication of the Tabernacle he was the first to bring his dedicatory offering. Nahshon was the ancestor of King David. They had a mixed Cushite origin and lived in Egypt for years. *Nathan* is mentioned in the New Testament in the genealogy section of Jesus of Nazareth, who is called the Messiah (Matthew 1:4 and Luke 3:32).

This means Nahson and his sister, *"Aaron's wife"* were also ethnic people and transferred their bloodline to **all** Priests and Temple ministers in the Levi tribe. His granddaughter Rehab was a **Hittite,** and she lived in a city called Jericho in the land of Moab. She hid the 2 spies that Joshua sent in to spy out the land before the Hebrews went in and took the land. **(Joshua 1-2).** The Moabites; descendants Moab [semitic Cushite] intermixed with Shelah; son of Judah's clans. The kinship between the Moabites and the Israelites is attested by the linguistic evidence of the **Moabite Stone**. The Moabites are also mentioned in close connection with the Amalekites, the inhabitants of Mount Seir, the Edomites, the Canaanites, the Sethites and the Philistines, and they all were people of color. All of the wonderful things that Yahweh directed to be made for his earthly house (temple) were made by these ethnic people. According to biblical scholars, the description of Shelah is an eponymous aetiological myth concerning fluctuations in the constituency of the tribe of Judah with Shelah representing the newest clan to become part of the tribe. The Book of Chronicles' description of Er as a descendant of Shelah, suggests that **Er** was in reality the name of a clan that was originally equal in status to Shelah. He was the son of the Canaanite woman *"Shudah";* who was the wife of Judah. Because of the scholars' attempt to hide the truth, I list the biblical and historical information in exact detail, so it's easily researchable. I don't want you to just take my words or totally deny this proof, "Study to show yourself approved" **2 Timothy 2:15**. The intellectuals have lied to you!

Hebron was a son of Kohath and grandson of Levi, and was the brother of Amram and the uncle of Aaron, Miriam and Moses. Hebron is portrayed in the text as the founder of the Hebronite faction of Levites. However, on some occasions, the Book of Chronicles treats the Hebronites as being ***distinct*** from the descendants of **Kohath**.

Eshtemoa was a town allotted to Judah and located in the mountains, (Joshua 15:50) that was given to the priests. (Joshua 21:1; 1 Chronicles 6:57). Hebron was one of the named places frequently visited by David and his followers during the long period of their wanderings (1 Samuel 30:28). These are the sons of Shelah; who was a son of Judah: Er; the father of Lecah, Laadah; the father of Mareshah and the clans of the house of linen workers at Beth-ashbea, Jokim and the men of Cozeba, Joash and Saraph who **ruled** in the city of Moab and returned to Lehem. These were the potters who were inhabitants of Netaim and Gederah. They lived there in the king's service. Two famous resident of Moab were Ruth and Rehab Nun 22:1. These people began to commit whoredom with the daughters of Moab Num 25:1. Moab was mixed with the clans of Judah's son Shelah, whose mother was a Canaanite woman [Shuah]. This black gene is connected to Jesus from Salmon-Rehab to Ruth and Boaz. Boaz was eighty and Ruth was forty years old when they married, and they were the parents of Obed; who was the father of Jesse; who was father of King David. King David had two sons [**Solomon and Nathan**], and both had a black gene lineage to **Salathiel**. Both Joseph and Mary [parent of Jesus] had a black gene lineage from Salathiel. This information is according to the genealogies chart in King James version of the 1611 Bible. Joseph was not Jesus' biological father; Yahweh was Jesus father by the Holy Spirit. According to the King James 1611 bible genealogies, Eli (also spelled Heli) was Mary's father and Joseph's Father-in-Law.

Nathan was the 3rd son of King David and Bathsheba and was historically incorrectly recorded; younger than Solomon. Solomon—Joseph is Matthew's recorded account and Nathan-Joseph (that should be to Mary) in Luke's recorded account. This information was erroneous translated either though transliteration or though translation of "**Father**" instead of "Father-in-Law". I'm not concerned with what method was used, only the fact that it is incorrect. The bible doesn't lie, so something happened to make both accounts different. Mary is Luke's account which is part of Jesus true genealogy. In Solomon-Joseph lineage there is a direct lineage, and with Nathan-Mary; it has several *"levirate"* marriages. This marriage is like Tamar's rights; Judah daughter-in-law **seed rights** (if a husband dies and have no male off spring, then his brother or near kinsmen must marry his widow and their offspring will become the decreased son or relative's offspring). This is not a theory, it is biblically sound. Nathan was a son born to King David and Bathsheba [both had black genes]. Some scholars say "He was the younger brother of Solomon", but 2 Samuel 5:14 list him before Solomon. Nathan is also mentioned to be the son of David in 2 Samuel 5:14, & 1 Chronicles 3:5 & 14:4.

✦ The Earth ✦

I continue to emphasize the color of these ancient ancestors, by doing so I'm revealing this bloodline was mixed into many people and nations creating a **world of color**. Solomon's declaration, "**I am Black**, but comely, O ye daughters of Jerusalem" **(Sol. I:5)**. Some scholars says this was an account of the bride's distinction and that assumption conflicts with the title of the Chapter, "Songs of Soloman", plus it conflicts with the black gene in his father and mother. Naamah, the wife of Solomon was an Ammonite [Lot's son Amman descendants] in which I have proven had black gene (Azurad, the wife of Eber and mother of Peleg and Joktan). Rehoboam; the son of Solomon married Maacah, daughter of his half brother Absalom; who was the son of King David from another wife.

Bathsheba, who was the mother of both Solomon and Nathan was the daughter of **Eliam**, one of David's "thirty mighty men" (2 Sam. 23:34; cf 1 Chr. 3:5). Eliam was the son of Ahitophel, one of David's chief advisors. Ahitophel was from **Giloh** (Josh. 15:51; 2 Sam. 15:12), which was a city in **Judah's** allotted land, and like King David, Bathsheba and her relatives were from the tribe of Judah that were mixed with Cushites.

Judah and his wives' descendants carried a mixture of Cushite and Canaanite genes. Consider the recorded history of intermixing that I have revealed and see the truth.

Bathsheba's family lineage possible intermixed with Ham's descendants numerous of times before Bathsheba's birth, and her marriage to King David. Uriah; the Hitite was Bathsheba's previous husband, and he was was one of King David's "mightly men" (39th) 2 Samuel 23. He was not considered cursed [Curse of Canaan] by King David, who knew Yahweh's teachings as some of the theologians have attested and lied stating, **"black skin is a curse."** Man is very proud and determined, **"I'll change the history books"**. Bath-**Sheba's** name originated from a Cushite named Sheba; the son of Raamah. This clan was formed in the Semitic civilization of **Saba** in Southern Arabia and Yemen, and they were known as the **Sabaeans**. Now note Shem's descendants originated from the same massive area as Ham's descendants and both nations worked together building the Tower of Babel. Israel's ethnicity is revealed in these bible verses; Lamentation 4:8, *their* visage (face) is **blacker** than coal. Lamentation 5:10, our skin was **black** like an oven. Job 30:30 states,

"My skin is **black** upon me." V5:7 say, "Our fathers have sinned and are not [they were dead], and we have borne their iniquities. Verse 5:7 is truly the reason I'm writing this book, "The pride of men with power and authority."

Raamah or Rama is a name found in the Bible that is first mentioned as the fourth son of Cush in Gen.10:7. Later this name appears as a country that traded with the Phoenician city-state of Tyre in Ezek. 27:22. It has been connected with Rhammanitae mentioned by Strabo in the southwest Arabian peninsula and with an Arabian city of Regmah at the head of Persian Gulf. The first Sheba was the nephew of King Nimrod; who founded several cities in Mesopotamia, including Babylon and Accad. We know from the inscriptions of ancient **Sheba**, Raamah's descendants settled near to the land of Havilah to the east of Ophir. This area was later ruled by Joktan's son named Sheba. This country of Raamah is usually assumed to be somewhere in the region of Yemen. Sheba was a son of Raamah and his descendants are often believed to be included amoung the **Sabeans.** The Yemenites are dark-skinned as are the descendants of their progenitor's eponymous grandfather, Kush or Cush, commonly translated in the bible as Ethiopia and some are *very dark-skinned people*. Dedan was the son of Raamah. His land was an apparent region of the Medina Province of Saudi Arabia. The Book of Jeremiah 25:16-25 states that the Hebrew *mingled* with the nations of Egypt, and all the kings of the land of Uz (Job, "The righteous" lived there). This ethnic mixing included the Philistines, Ashkelon, Azzah, Ekron, Edom, Moab, the children of *Ammon* [Lot sons]; Tyru, Zidon, *Dedan,* Tema, Buz, Zimri, and most of them lived in Arabia. **V29 of** Jeremiah states, "Ye shall *certainly drink* [mingle-mix]". Now look at the color of people that live in these areas today after 2000 years of intermixing with Caucasians, they are still all shades of color.

JUDGES 3:5 'and the children of Israel **lived** among the Canaanites, Hittites, and Amorites, and Perizzites, and Hivites, and Jebusites: . . . v3:6 "And they **took** their sons and daughters **in marriage**.'

All paintings and movies which we have seen have left imprints in our imagination and have made a false impression imprinted in our spirits and souls. All of those imprints have painted a lie into our spirit. I'm trying to convey Yahweh's feelings are not about a race of people, but his feeling about godliness and ungodliness, including excessive pride and deceit. High-minded men are the ones with this ungodly concept, **"I'm better than you"**. This isn't a race issue, but it is a spiritual pride issue. This reflects the spiritual nature of its father who stated, "I will ascend above the stars!" **Isaiah 14:13.** Remember pride is not a race issue, but a spiritual issue. Matthew 7:16 "By their fruit you will **recognize** them". All human beings are Yahweh's create children, but to be called "My Spiritual Children" by Yahweh, we have to obey His teachings of love. **John 13:35-John 8:44-45.** The true message I'm attempting to convey is that man is hopeless without God's guidance and His principle and directive is to **LOVE**, as God loves us. Jesus died for all of men's sins, every one of them. Yahweh is filled with love. We all can truly be "God's People" by asking God. After asking God, we wait for the "Love Doctor" to spiritually operate on us, spreading in us and though us; touching the world with His love. True love accomplishes all the things that it is set to accomplish. It will not return empty **Isaiah 55:11. Godly** Love is **not a feeling**; it is an action or reaction to an act of another. God's love does not require any motivation, only encouragement, because it is motivated by itself alone. Thereby, you can love anyone without an act from them that caused you to love. Love is self-motivated and it is just looking for a recipient. I pray that you benefit from reading this book, because it is written only to encourage and to lead someone that wants the best of this life and the life to come.

By revealing the true color of mankind ancestors, this information will possibly cause some to be offended, if so *offense is not intended*. To the person that is offended; As God commands all mankind to love; thereby I will do my part. Anyone should be able to voice their opinion about facts as they see them without offense. Historical and biblical records support these facts as I see it and these records reveal the ancient Hebrews (Israel) were a mixed race of color. All of the information in this book is biblically sound, every word, every thought, every opinion, and supported by historical facts only when biblical records do not. The historic records are used without contradicting any biblical record.

King James 1611 version bible genealogy chart support ethnicity was within Jesus family. **Simon**; the Canaanite [Zealot] was Jesus 1st Cousin. I know God's word instructs; "The fear of the Lord is the beginning of knowledge and fools *despise* wisdom and discipline" Proverbs 1:7. A biblical fool doesn't want any part of spiritual wisdom and spiritual wisdom cannot live with a fool. The worldly individual can have all types of university degrees and can be foolish spiritually. Our intellect cannot receive the wisdom of God 1 Corinthians 1:25. The intellect of man cannot believe that he has something **before** he can see it or touch it. God instructs Christians to have **Faith**. "Faith is the **substance** of things **hope for** and the **evidence** of things **not seen**" Hebrews 11:1. Most of God's revelations are spiritual discerned. The intellectuals call this discernment foolishness. Consider the statements that were made by Jeremiah Lamentation 4:8; "Their visage (face) is blacker than coal." **Lamentation 5:10.** Jeremiah was talking about "The precious sons (male and female) of Zion" and in v2 and v5:10 it states; "**Our** skin was **black** like an oven". There are many shades of black complexion and Jeremiah was saying, "I'm getting darker" as well as stating, "The precious sons of Zion" were ethnic ***Blacks***.

The true color of our ancestors is not depicted in today's paintings or image depictions and this truth has not been revealed in our history books. These biblical individuals were ethnic people and collectively forming nations, and we had lost our true history.

I believe every race or nation that has people of color originated from these men and women that were black-skinned. Prior to King David, Bathsheba was previously married to Uriah the Hittite, which was a sub-clan of Canaan. Canaan's father wasn't cursed making his **skin turn black** as some scholars attest. Canaan received the curse from Noah, so his father's skin was already black. This information proves the fact that scholars, historians and theologians intentionally excluded people of color from biblical history. These lies deprived numerous races of people from knowing their true history. The encouragement and motivation of this truth that would have brought strength to some of people that were enslaved by wealthy Caucasian men. This truth was hidden though the years due to the greed of a few wealthy men. This issue is not a race issue; it is the greed and ungodliness in man (main issue). As I've said before, "There are good people in every race and all Caucasians did not have knowledge of the truth, so they believed as they were told. "They are cursed to serve their brothers", by this misinformation, these misinformed Caucasians believed a lie. "I believe a lot of them were godly people and they thought they were performing a righteous act" Matthew 16:2. I truly believe; "This enslavement was God's will." Our ancestors [Hebrews] were **cursed** as with other Hebrews **for not obeying** God's Commandments.

Now consider both Holocausts, the Jewish holocaust and Black slavery, including other tragic events that happened to other races of color in light of the biblical prophecy and see the Truth Deuteronomy 28: 15-68. Now look at our US dollar and see the Egyptian Pyramid, with the same prophetical words and it indicates America is this Egypt. This was the Egypt prophesied in Deuteronomy 28; **"I'll send you by ships"**. The Jews weren't shipped to Europe to be imprisoned and slaughtered, they already were living there. The American Blacks in whom mixed as before into other races were shipped to North America, South America, Britain, Spain, France, and all of the American Islands. We can't get mad with a race of people that God had harden only a few of them for his purpose ROMAN 9:18. "I will have mercy on who

I will have mercy and harden, whoever I will **harden.**" Who can resist God in His anger? Man can only obey or disobey Him, and in disobedience Yahweh's purpose will not be changed.

No single race is not evil, nor is there any individual race good and godly. Remember Lucifer comes with God's Angels before him, and God asks him, "**Have you tried my servants?**" All humans tried this way so God can see who will obey His command to love all mankind. All things work out for the good to them who love God. Remember Jesus called a woman a dog? Matthew 15:22-28 Then look at God's spiritual principle with all incidents; including slavery and with any individual or group prerogative nature.

Remember this is not a White, Black, Hispanic or any other ethnic issue, it's a **pride and love** issue, and both can't live with each other. With that being said, in every negative action, there can be a positive result. It is all up to you to receive the positive gift from any act or incident. God says; "I must tear you down, before I can raise you up!"

God wants to see who will we **trust;** our eyes, **feelings** or **only** His holy words. How did the woman that was called a dog respond to her insult? Matthew 15:22-2*8*. She got what she wanted, plus she was finally complemented "**Great is thy faith!**" God says "Good will come from this" Romans 8:28. I believe God and hope you do too. So love your fellow man unconditionally John 13:35. No individual can tear you down, when you know who you are, and who you belong to. What does feelings have to do with believing Yahweh? He said "You are blessed", so you need to believe it.

At this point I have proven people of color lived in not only in Africa, but India, Turkey and mostly *all* of the **Middle East** as we know this land today. These were people of color, and we are today called many names, dark, Black or as in America "Afro-Americans." Old ancient maps show the borders of Africa, which covered the whole continent including additional countries. Egypt is part of the Continent of Africa and this fact is excluded in current present day acceptance as being a country of Africa. Now look at the King James 1611 bible genealogy chart and notice the ancient Egyptians are the descendants of **Mizarim;** who was the son of Ham; who was the father of the Black race. Yet the current leaders in Egypt states the black painting on the walls of the ancient Kings' tombs don't mean they were Blacks. See the pride in man? **"I'll change history."** Genesis 10:19 "The Canaanites extended from Sidon in the direction of Gerar as far as Gaza and in the direction of Sodom, Gomorrah, Admah, and Zeboiim, as far as Lasha." The Bible says the Canaanites weren't totally driven out of their land, but paid tribute to Israel. Additionally Joktan; who was atleast half Cushite and was the son of Eber and Azurad, and his land was not in Africa. America's history books states Afro-Americans came **only** from Africa, and that is not totally true. Joktan II; who was the son of Abraham and Keturah inherited the land right of his grandfather.

This land was later ruled by Joktan II with his two sons, Sheba and Dedan, including Joktan's five brothers. Joktan land was from Mesha as thou goest unto Sephar, a mount of the east according to Genesis 10:30. Ancient Mesha was located in **Arabia.** Medieval Arab genealogists divided the Arabs into two groups: the "original Arabs" of South Arabia, descending from Qahtan (identified with the biblical **Joktan**). The Easton's Bible Dictionary account for the land of Havilah, who was one of the son of the first man named Joktan and extended at least from the Persian to the Arabian Gulf. On account of its vast extent easily divided into two distinct parts. This land may have been Havilah's royal inheritance from the first Havilah; who was the son of Cush. Fausset's Bible Dictionary believes this view to be true and states, **"They became one people."**

CHAPTER 9

Ancient Egyptian Ethnicity

After Joseph became governor, his brothers and families were about 66-70 people when they entered Egypt. During his life and after his death, the Hebrew population in Egypt grew tremendously. Because of this growth, they were no longer looked upon as friendly neighbors. These Egyptians were of the **same ethnicity** as the Hebrews. The Egyptians decided they would impose upon them their own form of birth control. It sound like the same thing is going on in America today. "A bounce of takers and don't have any fathers around to take care of them. Their women are just having babies, while still being a baby themselves", are statements that are spoken often by media reports. "I know I'm touching a nerve, so find out who God say you really are and act accordingly." Anyone can have an opinion, but is that God's opinion? See what God says about the fruit of your womb or your mate's womb.

To keep the population of Hebrews in check, Pharaoh decreed that all Hebrew males be killed at birth (**Exodus 1**). This brings us directly to the story of Moses. Moses was born a Hebrew—Israelite from the tribe of Levi (**Exodus 2:1-3**). He spent 40 years in the house of Pharaoh (Acts 7:23) from the time he was an infant and passed as the Pharaoh's grandson **(Exodus 2: 6, 10)**. This was during the same time that Pharaoh ordered all Hebrew males under the age of two to be killed. By ignoring the previous command of Pharaoh, the mid-wives did not kill them at birth. After this failed, Pharaoh ordered the Egyptians to kill the Hebrew babies on sight. With the thought in mind, if Pharaoh was a black-skinned descendant of Ham, it would follow the course of the idea that Moses was black-skinned too. Consider Mered's influence; Pharaoh daughter's husband was Hebrew and this means he also was possibly Black or a man of color. **1 Chon. 4:18**. Some Scholars say the Pharaoh who was on the throne of Egypt at the time of Moses' birth was possibly **Seti I**, yet this is still ignored by most Historians. This King was the father of Rameses II, the Pharaoh of the oppression and he was also known as Rameses the Great.

George Rawlinson, an English author wrote a book entitled History of Egypt. On page 252, he gives a description of **Seti I** and he states: "King Seti's face was thoroughly **African**. He had a stormy face with a depressed flat nose, thick lips and heavy chin" (Notice the noses on most of all the ancient statues in Egypt are damaged. View them over the internet). Moses **had** to have the **same** physical characteristics because again, he was raised in the house of Pharaoh as the grandson of Pharaoh. Let's view this idea, if the Israelites were a very light or white-skinned people, how could Moses the Hebrew survive (secretly) in the house of Pharaoh among black-skinned Egyptians for 40 years and not be noticed as non-Egyptians? Impossible, after Pharoah gave the decree to kill all Hebrew males. How could Pharaoh face and rule over his people, if he knowingly had one living in his house with all the rights and privileges of his own family? Moses survived 40 years in the palace of Pharaoh because he was **a black-skinned man** just as the ancient Egyptians were. When Joseph and his wife Mary fled into Egypt, they fled among people who look like the couple and their child. There were no such Hebrew name "Mary", rather possibly Miriam and surely Yahushua. The ancient Egyptians of biblical times called their land and themselves Khemet, which in their tongue means

"The land of Blacks." The word Khemet is nothing but a variation on the word Khawm in the language of ancient Egypt. In Psalm 78:51, ". . . And smote all of the 1st born in Egypt, the tabernacle of Ham [khawm]." Psalm 105:23, 27 calls Egypt the land of Khawm [**Ham**], Verse 23 "Israel also came into Egypt and sojourned in the land of Ham; who was the father of the Black race.

Herodotus 484—425 BC was one of the most widely traveled individual of his time. His writings show his interest in both history and geography. Herodotus was born in Halicarnassus, a Greek colony in Asia Minor. He was a frequent visitor to Athens; he was a close friend of Sophocles. He also journeyed to the western shores of the Black Sea, to southern Italy and Egypt and to the Asian cities of Tyre, Babylon, Ecbatana, Nineveh and Susa, and noted in the Compton's Interactive encyclopedia. During his travels, Herodotus kept a journal of his activities. The journal was later translated and in one of his entries, he wrote the following about the Egyptians or to be more exact the natives: "It is certain that the natives of the country are **Black**; there can be no doubt that the **Colchians** are an Egyptian race. I made this inquiry on the subject both in Colchis and in Egypt and I found that the Colchians had a more distinct recollection of the Egyptians, than the **Egyptians had of themselves**. My own conjectures were founded, first, on the fact that they are black-skinned and have **woolly hair**. With that analogy the ancient Egyptians and the Hebrews were of the same ethnicity."

Dr. Yosef A. A. Ben-Jochannan; who is an Ethiopian Jew states, "These African Hebrews, as all other Romanized-African of this era, were caught in a *rebellion in Cyrene* (Cyrenaica) during 115 C.E. against Roman imperialism and colonialism. Some of these Hebrews had previously migrated to Cyrene after the Roman siege of Jerusalem in the year 70 AD." Josephus, an ethnic Jewish historian, was sent to negotiate with these Hebrew defenders. Josephus described these Hebrews as ethnic people in "Antiquities of the Jews." This rebellion also marked the beginning of a mass Jewish **migration southward** into Soudan [Sudan or West Africa] along the way of the city Aer (Air) and into the countries of Futa Jalon and Senegal [Sene-Gambia] which lie below the parabolic curve of the Niger River's most northern reaches, where the City of Tumbut [Timbuktu, Timbuctoo], Melle [Mali] presently stands" This is written in "African Origins of the Major Western Religions, 1970, p. 76". Dr. Ben goes on to relate that Black Israelite immigrants from northern and eastern Africa merged with indigenous groups in western Africa to become the Fulani of Futa Jalon, Bornu, Kamen, and Lake Chad. They also formed the *parent-stock* of groups such as the Ashanti, the Hausa, the B'nai *Ephraim,* and the Bavumbu [Mavumbu or Ma-yomba]. All of these groups suffered tremendous population decreases during the years the *Atlantic slave trade* was in operation, others were completely eliminated". The B'nai Ephriam tribe is identified by the biblical name "Ephriam" Joseph half-Egyptian son. All of our ancestors did not come from Africa; they **migrated** there during 115-114 C.E. Look at the history of these people and look at the wars today and the adverse affects that the wars cause people migrate to safety, so they think. The "Out Post" Tribal Leaders weren't enslaving their people; they had plenty of **immigrants** to sell.

Critics claim Dr. Ben is anti-Semitic because some of the statements he has made and they really don't have a true claim to this unwarranted criticism. Dr. Ben ethnic nation [Ethiopians] has been *recognized* as an Ethiopian Hebrew tribe by the government of Israel. Don't his critics have very proud belief? An acknowledged Jew is termed as anti-Semitic because of his knowledge of intermixing of the Hebrew tribes and how they migrated to Africa with no merit to prove their contention is valid or even reasonable. Jews are calling another Jew anti-Semitic, how is this possible? Does it have to do with **skin color**? I hope not, but pride is the only other answer I can ration. Pride is a biblical sin; this fact is noted in the Old Testament. Now consider this, the Jewish Eastern Orthodox Old Testament has 51 books, which covers all of the Old Testament in the American Bible. The Tanakh [Jewish Bible] contain 24 books and covers all of the American Old Testament. So why there is no knowledge within them reckoning pride as a sin? You figure it out, but some people that calls themselves righteous is evaluating themselves from their own doctrine and not according to the word of God. Philippians 2:3, "Esteem your brother greater than yourself." Proverbs 21:2 states, "A person may think their own ways are right, but the LORD weighs the heart". So God's word should be the judge of our reasoning and we are to do it with love. "Pride goes before destruction and a haughty spirit before a fall" **Proverbs 16:18**.

I'm not judging anyone's faith; I'm judging their acts according to their own faith doctrine. All professed Christians acts aren't according to our faith either. Remember, I stated; "Any faith or religious person can make it to Heaven by living a life of **Love** and this is biblical doctrine [Old or New Testament]. John 13:35 One may say, "The bible says; "You are not to judge." There are numerous verses stating; "Judge fairly and with justice" **Zechariah 8:16,** Leviticus 19:15, Deuteronomy 16:18, and finally 1 Corinthians 6:3. People who quote this one verse "**Do not judge**" are spiritually unlearned in Christ doctrine and do not **fully** know most biblical doctrine. Those that say this are giving their opinions, but Christians are taught to live only by **every word** that proceeds out of the mouth of God. We can't live by opinions, yet be careful with this freedom because with the measure you judge, you will be judged, so judge with caution Matthew 7:2. Notice I mentioned the act and did not identify the person. If that one verse was true, a Minister could not preach or teach, because in doing so; they are judging the acts and the people. I'm talking about sin in anyone as God has directed, word for word. Yahweh's teachings on any subject are to everyone. You will see in this book I've admitted my faults and God's corrections. I'm calling no names, unless it an intentional lie; it not about an individual, it's about the acts of people. If God's word hits anyone in the eye, well God is almighty, who can fight against His truth? I know I can't, I've tried Him! I've found out God is almighty!

Thereby I want this to be known, "I'm not criticizing any religion that is season in love", just their personal acts that is not according to their own faith or teachings. I was ordained to win souls, not to offend believers of God, atleast not intentionally. I say these things because of **MALACHI 4** which states, "Your words have been **stoud** against me, saith the Lord". What words? Anything you say, that is not season with love and respect. In all faiths there are sacred books that gives moral guidance and the Bible tell Christians to repent when we fail with God's Commandments. Therefore I respect all faiths, religions, all beliefs when they are **tempered** with **love** because God is the one who will separate and finally judge and reward. Let's continue with the history of man:

The new Pharaoh that had forgotten the good deeds of Joseph in Exodus 1:11 was possibly identified, "The other city he built was **Ramses**." The bible notes Pithom is one of the cities which according to Exodus 1:11, that was built for the Pharaoh of the oppression that started forced labor [slavery] of the Israelites. Egypt reached the pinnacle of its power during the New Kingdom in the Ramesside period where it rivaled the Hittite Empire, Assyrian Empire and Mitanni Empire, after which it entered a period of slow decline. This name Ramses lived for many hundreds of years though his descendants' rule. Menpehtyre Ramesses I or possible his son Seti I was the "New King" mentioned in Exodus 1:8. I contend no later than Ramesses II, who reigned 1279 BC-1213 BC of the Nineteenth dynasty. He is often regarded as the greatest, most celebrated and most powerful pharaoh of the Egyptian Empire. His successors and latter Egyptians called him the "Great Ancestor." Ramesses II led several military expeditions into the Levant, re-asserting Egyptian control over Canaan. Noted later in the Bible, Tharaca, who was the opponent of Sennacherib is called King of Ethiopia in 2 Kings 19:9 and Isaiah 37:9 and hence is not given the title Pharaoh which he bears in Egyptian documents.

CHAPTER 10

Prophecy of the Fate of Israel

Our Hebrew ancestors did not obey Yahweh and He replied to them in Deuteronomy 28:48 "I'll put a yoke of **iron upon thy neck,** until I have destroyed thee". Records estimates possibly multiple millions of slaves died before and after the slave trades. These Deuteronomy warnings are not metaphors conveyed in biblical teachings by scholars and theologians; it is literally happened, just as it was **prophesied.** This wasn't a Hamic curse in which Caucasians' property owners justified slavery. This was a direct Hebrew cruse for being **disobedient** to Yahweh. Deuteronomy 28:68' "The Lord shall bring thee into Egypt again with **ships** by the way whereof I speak unto thee". Notice the Egyptian pyramid on our US dollar. Even the Native Americans, South Americas and Mexican-Hispanics had to come by ships and all experienced tragic events in their history. All living beings descended from eight people after the flood and the next 4 to 5 generations were bore by family members that had married and produced offsprings from their families' members. Read all Deuteronomy Chapter 28 and understand what God's words say about our blessings once we obey and *return* to Yahweh. "I'm married to the backslider" **Jer 3:1.** The ancient Hebrew would put on sack cloth and ash [a symbolic; a true

✦ THE EARTH ✦

sorrowful devotion] and cry out to Yahweh! **Jonas 3:5 Jeremiah 6:26.** We really don't have to do this, just being sorrowful is enough. We shouldn't complain and say we haven't been treated right. The problem with man when he's wronged or feel wronged, he want to repay. This is not how Yahweh wants us to live, but live only by His biblical principles. Deuteronomy 28:13 concludes, "Which I command you this day to observe and to *do them*". Humans are not prefect, therefore Yahweh sent us His Son, who most Americans calls Jesus and he forgives all mankind for their sins. This forgiveness is only to those that follow Him. Man has a choice and he has a free will to make this biblical required choice.

One of America's first Holy Bibles were printed in 1611, the King James version was readable during the height of slave ownership. Biblical quotes supported these men [traders and owners] justification of slavery, but they ignored other biblical commands. Yahweh gave commandments about slavery even if you consider slavery was just or not. Yes, Yahweh knew men would be enslave, so He gave them directives to this unmoral issue **Deuteromy 15:12-18**. Those professed Christians slave owners also forgot or ignored Deuteronomy 15:12-18 "serve 7 Years and be freed", additionally the biblical **"Year of Jubilee"**. This was Yahweh's guidance to whoever owned slaves. The Jubilee year is the year at the end of seven cycles of shmita (Sabbatical years) and according to biblical directives, the Holy writing had a special impact on the ownership and management of land and slave ownership in the Land of Israel. There is some debate whether it was the 49th year [the last year of seven sabbatical cycles, referred to as the Sabbath's Sabbath], or whether it was the following 50th year. Jubilee deals largely with land, property and property rights. As with most cultures, the property rights regarding land, slaves and indentured servants was less absolute than for other property rights such as for tools and personal artifacts. How many hundreds of years the Blacks were enslaved in America?

It really doesn't matter, because this is my point; The Egyptians enslaved these Hebrews for 400 years and those were our [same family of Ham and his son; Mizriam] own brothers. Some scholars in Egypt today still claims these ancient Egyptian wasn't black. Their Tombs wall are painted with black faces and their status are Black. Yes, these scholars say it a symbol of fertility and the ancient historians writing don't agree with that idea. They were descendants of Miziriam; son of Ham, who was the Father of the Black race. All things in life **are** about how we react to people actions. Can you see its not about a race and its only about pride; which is a sin? You would only know this if you knew the teachings of Yahweh. God's teachings are about an individual's reactions to all things and God's commandment is to love them [offenders] regardless to the fact that love is not given or returned.

This issue of Slavery; have this happen before? Yes, numerous times, but I'll emphasized my point with Joseph, the son of Jacob/Israel. His own biological brothers sold him into slavery. Thereby slavery is not about a race of people, but Godliness or ungodliness, including God hardening hearts to accomplish His mission. After years of slavery passed; Joseph became governor over all of Eygpt. God allowed this to happen; as He has allowed Black slavery to happen. This included the omission of our Black history. By doing so, Yahweh proved some men are "ungodly" and to prove that **all** men need His guidance to be righteous and to be morally sound. This was also to punish us for not obeying Him under the Law [Commandments]. Some might be offended by my statements, but I'm doing what I was directed by God. Some Blacks might say; "This is not a Godly message", if so, it reveals you lack biblical teachings. Read your bible and see Yahweh in His anger. Learn to trust Yahweh and you wouldn't have to fear Him, *"I am a jealous God!"* Exodus 20:5 Yahweh says what He means and means what he says. The scriptures also shows the hearts of wicked men when Blacks were enslaved using biblical quotes. Deuteronomy also stated, "Visiting the iniquity of the fathers upon the children unto the third and fourth generation". Slavery lasts in Egypt and again in America more than 3 to 4 generations.

Since most Blacks believe slavery was a Caucasian's sin, look at this fact: Anthropologist, Count Constatin de Volney (1727-1820), spoke about the race of the Egyptians that produced the Pharaohs. He later paid tribute to Herodotus' discovery when he said: "The ancient Egyptians were **true Negroes** of the same type as **all** native born **Africans**. With that being so, we can see how their blood *mixed* for several centuries with that of the Romans and Greeks, must have lost the **intensity** of it's original color, while retaining none the less the imprint of its original mold. We can even state as a general principle that the face [The Sphinx] is a kind of monument able, in many cases, to attest to, or shed light on historical evidence on the origins of the people. The fact that the ancient Egyptians were black-skinned prompted Volney to make the following statement: "What a subject for meditation, just think that the race of Black men today our slaves and the object of our *scorn*, is the very race to which we *owe* our **arts**, *science* **and even the use of our speech**." Wake up and know who you are! The testimony of the ancients, the Bible, many Egyptologists, along with archeologists confirmed that the Egyptians during biblical times were black-skinned people. So remember Blacks had their hands in slavery, so slavery isn't a race issue, it an power and pride issue.

The painting of Pyramid tombs in Ethiopia and Sudan **has** the identical style writings as the ancient Egyptians on their walls and these ancient people of Sudan were Black. I'm not trying to cause any violence or rebellion against our authorities. I say this because of the racial tension in America today. I believe all people of color need to know their history. The content of this book is meant only to inform, encourage and not inflame. **Titus 3:1 "Remind** the people to be subject to rulers and authorities, to be **obedient**, to be ready to do whatever is **good**". Promoting rebellion or being rebellious isn't a godly trait; it is spiritually demonic and comes from its father (The one that was kicked out of Heaven). The ones that promote such acts are *known* by the fruit that they produce.

This was why I spoke earlier against the behavior of our white Jewish brothers calling Dr. Yosef A. A. Ben-Jochannan, an Ethiopian

Jew; anti-semitic and his critics statements against him had no spiritual or moral judgment in them. Dr. Yosef is an acknowledged Jew. This individual assumption [anti-semitic theory] is like telling a preacher he cannot preach against sin. When anyone has sinned; the words of Yahweh are directed to Him, individually and to all, with no respect of person. I'm attempting to convey the love that Yahweh has for all mankind; including all ethnicities. I say these things because fleshly man loves to hate and hates to love. So let no offense be caused by the truth as I see it and I will support what I'm writing with traceable evidence [biblical and historical writings]. If you still don't believe in what I'm stating, you have a right to do so. This is one of your rights by being an American or your native country right. In sayings that; shouldn't I also have that same right to convey my findings in writing without intentional offense? I was ordain to win souls, not to intentionally offend souls. Therefore if you are offended by these recorded facts, they were collectively written with this thought; "I will not cause intentional offense, I'm just conveying God's message as he inspires me to do so". I attempting to bring back spiritual Israel to the love of God **without claiming rights to a land,** because our home really is in Heaven [Heaven on Earth], after Jesus returns. I'm attempting to prepare you [Yahweh's People] in this journey to our heavenly home in which I believe will be here on Earth at the End of Times. Thereby I continue in this attempt:

We know the all Blacks are not "godly", nor all ungodly, this fact is proven by God saying "You are not my people", and again "You are my beloved". Godliness can only be attained through acceptance and obedience to Jesus. In this act [obedience] of life, any person can be one of God's people, "Whosoever calls upon my name, *shall be saved*" **Rom. 10:13**—meaning if we are "Godly people", we must love in judgment in our normal daily lives. Race, money or power does not have anything to do with salvation. But pride, "I'm better than you"; this attitude will keep you from Yahweh salvation. Proverbs 16:18-19 "Pride goes before destruction and a haughty spirit before a fall". I see when most minority groups have *professed* this truth; the media (which is white owned) states; "Possibly a hate group". Maybe, but on the other hand, for the media to say this and know our slavery history; is like a German telling an acknowledged Jew, "You are not Jews" and stop talking about the Holocaust; we are *tired* of you using the "Jew Card". Look at the pride of Man.

The Atlantic slave traders that ordered by volume were: the Portuguese, the British, the French, the Spanish, the Dutch and the Americans. They had established outposts on the African coast where they purchased slaves from local African tribal leaders(remember our ancestors did the same thing to their own brother Joseph). With that said, afterward our ancient Black brothers (Egypt) did it again and kept our ancestors enslaved for hundreds of years before this enslavement in America. Additionally, the out post in Africa had the okay with the Tibal Lords, which was our African ancestors learning their old ways again. Current estimates are that about 12 million were shipped across the Atlantic to America and Americas Islands, although the actual number purchased by the traders is considerably higher. The slave trade is sometimes called the Maafa by African and African-American scholars, meaning "great disaster" in Swahili. Some historic scholars, such as Marimba Ani and Maulana Karenga, use the terms "***African Holocaust***" or "Holocaust of Enslavement". I contend the Native Americans had their Holocaust or history of genocide, as well as the Mexicans and South Americans today. Too many innocent people are being gunned down in mass numbers. Historical records show they were possibly of the tribe of Dan or Asher or one of the other 10 lost tribes.

I've heard this statement so many times; "**Stop using the Black Card**". I really don't know what that "Card" contains. I feel deep sympathy for the Jewish and Native American holocausts victims and their families. In addition; I'm sympathetic to my Black brothers and sisters that have lost their lives during and after the slave trade and **struggling** to find themselves after slaves have been long ago freed. I contend in fairness; all of the true biblical history should be made known [this is what I'm attempting]. All minorities are not takers or on welfare as we have been termed by the media. With knowing biblical history, some are still proud that these events happened. There are many proud people on earth and our ancestors had this proudness also. They harden their hearts and would not received the words from God. Yahweh responded; Deuteronomy 28:62 "You shall be left a *few in number*, where as you were as the *stars* of heaven for *multitude*" Now considered what the recorded historical evidence have proven; People of color not only lived in Africa, but India and mostly **all** of the Middle East as we know it day. Our ancestors were great in numbers as the stars of the universe. Before you get angry and sin; continue to listen to Yahweh about anger, proudness and stubbornness.

Deu. 28:48 "Therefore shalt thou *serve* thy enemies which the Lord shall send against thee, in hunger, and in thirst, and in nakedness, and *want of* all things: and he shall put a yoke of iron upon thy neck until he have ***destroyed*** thee". Who spoke these bad things? Look again; The Lord God! Who can fight against Him? Remember He is almighty. Then what should we do? Repent and ask for mercy and return your heart to God; we have seen His power. This enslavement literally happened as the bible stated [prophesied]. Do you see that the white Jews received their punishment (Europe)? This wasn't and isn't a race issue. Amos 9:9 I will command and I will sift the house of Israel among **all** nations, like as corn is SIFED in a sieve, yet shall not the last grain fall upon the earth. V10 All the sinners of my people shall die by the sword, which say, The evil shall not overtake nor prevent us. In God's anger, the destroyer [Lucifer] is loosed and God will ask, "Have you tired my servant that serves me only when he **feels** like serving me?" Lucifer have and will again respond, "I'll have them cursing and walking away from you [God], plus cursing and mistreating your other servants in just a few minutes." If your relationship is close with God; you are not in this number, if you are; turn you hearts back to your Creator. Learn your benefits for returning to Yahweh; read the words of Yahweh and obey.

✦ The Earth ✦

This is God's promise on your return; Micah 7:19 "He will turn again, He will have **compassion** upon us; He will subdue our iniquities v20 "Thou wilt perform the truth of Jacob, and the **mercy** to Abraham, where he has sworn unto our fathers from the days of old". Micah 5:3 "Then the remnant [a set number] of his brethren shall return unto the children of Israel [God's people]." Remember people of color are part of Israel and don't let no one tell you different. God's children **have** a promise upon returning; a blessing we can't imagine. **We do not need land in Israel**, Heaven is our home, including all the blessings the God has promised for us on this earth. Remember the protocol son and with this truth, remember **God's grace**. Luke 15:11-32. With this remembrance of his grace; encourage yourself in Yahweh's goodness and grace and learn to love and forgive the way our Lord want you too. Man might hate you, but Yahweh loves you and commands you to love all men, including those haters. "I'm the good shepherd; the good shepherd give his life for his sheep". John 10:11 Jesus did it, He died for our sins, not for his sin; but for the sins all mankind. So will you give your life to him? This is the way we give our life; by changing the way we think and act; "**Dying to self**" as the bible states in Mark 8:34-35, Luke 9:23-24. If we are not willing to make this change; Jesus says, "You are not worthy of me" Mat 10:38. Therefore our White brothers and sisters shouldn't suffer our hate, but only enjoy our love.

Now remember, when anyone *suppresses* biblical truths for whatever reason, they are biblically identified; "Enemies of Yahweh", by not receiving God's truth. Blacks' history is part of that truth, as well as other people of color. "You are of your *father* the devil and the lusts of your father ye will do" John 8:44'45, Jesus was talking to Hebrew Scholars/priests because they had ungodliness in them. So saying you are a Christian, Jew or whatever faith you are, that proclamation doesn't make you righteous. But by the act of love; it **identifies you**. Whoever erased our history will have their reward, whoever fights against the truth will have their reward and whoever doesn't listen to the truth will have their reward. Read the verses

I've listed in this book and come to your own conclusion. God loves and I'm commanded to love you too, therefore be encouraged. Why do I love you? Because my Father loves you and told me; **Love all people**; especially those of my house [the house of Faith].

Those that have an ear let him or her hear and come to accepting the truth of Yahweh. God overlooked our ignorance about these things in earlier times, but now He commands everyone, everywhere to repent for their sins and turn to Him. **Acts 17 :31**: "For He has set a day for **judging** the world with justice by the man He has **appointed** and He proved to everyone who this is by raising Him from the dead"; Jesus is his name as Americans know it. Remember what God *promised Abram*; "I'll bless those who bless you, but I'll curse the one who curses you and through you all the people of the earth will be blessed."(Genesis 12:3). Therefore why put yourself between God cross hairs by hating? Love, and do it with joy, just because God said it. He's awesome, wonderful and mighty in strength and a rewarder of them that seek him. God becomes angry sometime, but He is full of mercy. Some people might think Yahweh is evil by allowing bad things to happen. I know we all have heard someone say those words. Now read Jeremiah 24:5 **"I'm doing this for their good"** Jeremiah 25:12 "Afterward, I will punish them which came against my people". Remember you are not the only one God considers "My People", so be careful how you treat anyone.

Here is how Yahweh feel about the ones that say He is not fair if he let bad things happen; Rom. 9:18 'He have mercy on whom He will have mercy and whom He will he harden. V19. You will say then unto me, why doth He yet finds fault? v20 Oh man, *who art thou that replies against God?* Shall the *thing* (yes that is what God called you) formed say to Him that formed it, why has you made me so? v21. Have not the "potter power over the clay; of the same lump to make "one vessel unto honor and the other to dis-honor? What if God, willing to show his wrath, and to make his *power known*, **endured** with much long-suffering "the vessels of wrath" fitted to destruction. v23 And that He might *make known the*

✦ The Earth ✦

riches of his glory on the vessels of mercy, which He had previously **prepared** unto glory". We have a city and a home to go too. I believe every word of Yahweh. Those others mystical gods that are written about in books; none of them are like Yahweh; that loves, forgives, cleans, sanctifies and empowers normal men to do the things he does. All you have to do is say Jesus here I am; take me, **mold me** into your image. You are too good to be true, but I will trust you. I trust what your words say; "You can not lie" Num. 23:19. **I must** love and forgive, even when I don't **feel** like doing it. Remember; what do feelings have to do with believing and trusting Yahweh? This is the key to the door that we need to enter "The City of Gold." This is why I'm not offended or mad about the slavery issue or how minorities are treated today. For all things work to the good of them who loves the Lord. Romans 8:28

I believe as I forgive, my sins are forgiven me. Joseph wasn't mad at his brothers, yes, he played on his brothers' emotions that enslaved him emotions by charging them with thief, he really wasn't mad is a destructive sense Gen. 50:17-21. Joseph learned his imprisonment/slavery was directed by Yahweh to keep his people from starving to death Gen 45:5. There are possibly numerous reasons why human beings were enslaved and treated as they are today. One for sure; God wants to separate the lovers from the haters and give them a chance for repentance, because you are known by the fruit you bare. Matt. 7:16. Let your love shine forth regardless of what happened in the past or will happen in the future. I will ask you this question, how is a diamond made? First, it is a simple worthiness rock of coal that was pressured for many years. If you follow the guidance of Yahweh; a diamond is what you will become. Consider all the historical data; the ancient writings, prints and painting on stones depicting a race of color. If you don't own a computer, go to your library and research this, the truth can stand the test of scrutiny and pass it will flying colors.

PART 2

God's Love and Guidance

CHAPTER 11

God's Truth (Love)

God's grace is unto all men and He has given guidance in all things; especially how we treat each other. "Love you brother as yourself" and to "Love your enemy". God gave guidance even for slavery; because He knew man's heart was cold. Yahweh overall guidance to "all mankind" is to come back to being just and seek to be merciful and have Godly judgement in our thinking. This information is not to invite hate or to say "People of color are part of God's **true Hebrews**", this would take away the true meaning of God's message that I'm trying to convey.

If we hate White men or women for enslaving us what are we proving? Remember "People of color **invented slavery**" and we sold our own brothers. The the most famous was Joseph. God loves all of mankind and no single race is better than the others. But to those Hebrew descendants who are thinking or acting out as they are nothing or being rebellious to authority, even sometimes with justification; as the world knows justification. They truly have a need, they don't know spiritual love and that need can and will be fulfilled upon acceptance of Yahweh's grace. Therefore be encouraged, you are somebody and God will show you that you belong to Him; either in anger or in love, it's really your choice. To those Blacks that will read this and will become angry, **endue** the **will** of Yahweh, "All things happen for the **good** for them that loves the Lord". Things we can't understand sometimes will work out for our good. There are numerous biblical verses to tell you what your outcome with be and one of those "You are Blessed" Matthew 5:10. Thereby, just being honest and causing no harm or crime is a righteous act. I've lived and learn one main lessen about fleshly man; "He loves to hate" and "He" includes Blacks. This book is not for the purpose of promoting hate. Hate needs no encouragement; it is motivated all by itself. "Love covers a multitude of sin"1 Peter 4:8. Therefore Love needs all the encouragement that one can give and this book is only meant to motivate love [Agapa]. So even when men hate you or anyone close to you; you must show love. God loves them too [haters], whomever they are.

Agapa love is an action and it is **not a feeling** as mankind's **philio-love**. "Love only them that love you, let's make love, I like you", that is fleshly man love. Agapa love is why I can forgive, even when I don't feel like doing it. I know that I must forgive and I learn to let it go [whatever the problem is] with Yahweh's help. Spiritual lacked man thought forgiveness had to felt in their hearts, but this idea lack spiritual understanding. True love (agape), which is part of forgiveness and is not a feeling, it is **an act**. All we have to do is forgive, regardless of how bad the issue is or angry we are about the issue, submitting ourselves to Yahweh's Word; "Forgive and it will be forgiven to you". My sins, my unrighteousness will be forgiven with the **measure** that I forgives others.

This is Yahweh's message; If I forgive a little, I'm forgiven a little by him. In every negative action, God have a positive gift or positive development from it. After we have endured by believing in Yahweh's promises, we come out stronger than before.

I have to forgive, because I have a lot of sin written in Yahweh's book and I have to have mercy to enter his kingdom. Therefore forgiving you for wronging or hurting me is rewarded with what we knew as children "brownie points" with Yahweh. So when God's Angels open his book of **all** my recorded acts; I can stand before

✦ THE EARTH ✦

Him and ask; "Mercy God, please have mercy on me" and the measure of mercy I have given in this life will be measured to see if it covers all of my sins. This is a simple truth. Now remember every negative bring a positive, therefore we can endure mistreatment, endure sufferings, endure people doing wrong to us, because; "I need mercy and plenty of it" Matthew 5:7. This is why our ancestors couldn't totally understand Yahweh, because our leaders (Prophets and Priests) became crooks; wicked men and afterward; the people became lackful in spiritual food and strayed from God's spiritual teachings and they became rebellious. Notice what happened when the Levite Priests defiled themselves.

Lev. 10:1 And Nadab and Abihu, the sons of Aaron, took either of them his censer and put fire therein and put incense thereon and offered strange fire before the LORD, which he commanded them not. Yahweh told them in detail how to perform what some men call a primitive-barbaric ritual, but to maturely informed Christians, it was Spiritual. We are under a New Covenant today and don't have to sacrifice like that anymore, that debt of Law have been paid in full by Jesus/Yahushua's blood. 10:2 And there went out fire from the LORD and devoured them and they died before the LORD. 10:3 Then Moses said unto Aaron, This is it what the LORD Spoke, saying, I will be sanctified in them that come nigh to me before all the people and I will be glorified. And Aaron held his peace. Even when his sons had died, **Aaron was in peace**. Aaron was at peace because he learned this incident was Yahweh's will. So whatever state or situation we are in, we can be at peace and glorify Yahweh for just being God. He is awesome, almighty and we must be humble before Yahweh and realizes as Aaron did; **"Yahweh knows his business"**. Yahweh wants to be glorified in every situation, even if we don't have a job, no money, can't make ends meet; we should remember this is God/Elohim! When we have endured, keep on looking for work as long as it takes, Yahweh will eventually bless, money will come and our responsibilities [bills] will be met and Yahweh will still be glorified, just because he is God. All we have to do is **believe** in God, because Yahweh will never fail us. But, we will fail His guidance. We stop looking for work, start complaining and what happens? We *lose hope*. "Hope deferred makes the heart sick" Proverbs13:12. If Yahweh words say it; He knows it and cannot lie, so you are not at your breaking point. If your petition doesn't happen right away, be encouraged, Yahweh is always on time!

"Great is the LORD and most worthy of praise; His greatness no one can fathom" (Psalm 145:3). "I call to the LORD, who is worthy of praise and I am saved from my enemies" (2 Samuel 22:4). To some Christians; this is foolish rumble, but read your bible and find out the truth and you will see those that think this way are like our brothers that wondered in the wilderness. Moses asked "Who is on Yahweh side" and all of them that loved Yahweh started moving toward Moses and the rest were consumed by the earth. This literally happened; the earth opened up and *swallowed* those unbelieving haters Numbers 16:31-32. Read this book and follow the referenced verse in the bible and see the truth, Yahweh has not changed; we [the church] have.

When you find yourself, as it is said, *"Down and out"*, bring you petitions before Yahweh, *Plead you case*! Micah 6:1, Jeremiah 12:1, Jeremiah 42:**9**. Maybe Yahweh wants to know how much you remembered His spiritual words about His mercy and goodness. Say them or quote them; even if you have to find them and read them *directly* out of the bible, but it is better if you can get them in your spirit where they will roll out like water rolling over a rock. I guarantee; if you continually read those [Holy Words], they will come to your memory when you need them. I know God will never fail you. I know Yahweh will give you the desires of your heart as long as they are Godly. Don't misunderstand this truth, Yahweh will not give you another man's wife, nor husband, nor house. He will give you your own *unclaimed;* not owned by another desire. We have to bring our thoughts in line with holiness and godliness. There are plenty empty houses and plenty single women and men (that if you are not married already).

1 Peter 1:23 (NIV) "Now that you have *purified* yourselves by *obeying* the truth so that you have *sincere love* for your brothers,

love one another deeply, from the heart. For you have been *born again*, not of perishable seed, but of imperishable.

"Forgive, and you shall be forgiven."

So If I do good, good will follow me, if I'm wicked, wickedness will follow me. If I bless, blessings will follow me and if I forgive, forgiveness will follow me. Then no matter how I *feel*, if I truly believe Yahweh's words (I do), I see that I can be blessed while enduring *any* situation, just by following (trusting) the way of truth [God's written words]. Thereby, I cannot hold onto **anger, strife and hate,** because they rob me of of my blessings from Yahweh. These biblical words are personal, and then again directed to all mankind. I can't control my situation, but I can trust in what the Lord say, instead of what I **feel or think.** "What do Yahweh say on this issue?", should be our question on every simple issue in life. Thereby, I can forgive and do it with haste, because unforgiveness is a blessing's robber and I want all of my blessings. Do you want all of your blessings?

To love like this (agape love), First, I'll pray to Yahweh with King David's prayer; in his prayer he petitions God, "**Create** in me a clean heart and give me a steadfast spirit" Psalms 51:10. King David had sinned by not only taking another man's wife, but killing him to get her. See how Yahweh forgives? I want to be steadfast in trusting Yahweh words and those bad feelings will go away. Remember man loves to hate. A spiritual **operation** has to happen with some issues, therefore I'll ask my God, "**Create in me**"; this operation is better than a doctor's operation, "It's Spiritual", meaning my God's **hand is on me.** I petitioned God and I know He will answer my prayer and do whatever I ask. Why? Just because He said "I will bless you". So my sincere petition is enough in itself, just by asking and knowing God will do what is good for me to find rest-peace with the issue at hand. Matthew 7:7 and John 16:23.

"My people are destroyed, because of the lack of knowledge" Hosea 4:6. This wasn't and still isn't presently, a common intellectual knowledge, but only a Godly spiritual knowledge for His people. We are not destroyed by the White man or held down by him. No man can't be hold down God's true believer! These negative feelings and acts are not about the color of one skin, it is about the **content of one's heart**. Yahweh ways and guidance are foolish to fleshly man. Yahweh's response is not always going to be **sweet**, readily acceptable by us, sometimes His words are sharper than a two edge sword, but this is God. Remember, He is awesome, almighty, all-knowing, merciful, but He can't be defeated. So give up you can't win against Him! Learn about Jesus' statements and actions with the woman that petitioned Him for her need and Jesus called her a ***dog*** and her response was; "Yes, Lord, yet even the little **dogs eat** the crumbs which fall from their *masters'* table **Matthew 15:27**. Jesus responded back to her, "**Great is thy faith!** Most Christians today would have been insulted, "I know he didn't call me a dog", and walked away without what they needed. But this woman saw it another way, "I will not trust my **feelings** of being insulted, this man is Jesus and I've heard of his power. I'm not leaving until I get what I ask, so **I'll *humble*** myself before him". Didn't she get what you wanted? Some people want to be lifted high, but Yahweh say, "Before I can lift you up, I have to bring you down and see who or what (feelings?) you will **trust**". Do you see what God has done with the negative impression that people have about people of color? This included some minorities with this pride "I'm better than your attitude." We trust our feelings too much! Will you be lifted up? Then humble yourself before God; He will see and He will be waiting for you ask for anything that fits a godly purpose. Let your heart receive this godly message.

Remember what is going on in the world is Yahweh's will and His words are Life; His words are living-tangible and if you receive and accept them, they are powerful in strengthening you, growing you in maturity of his Faith. Thereby, when we speak, the world elements respond like it's God Himself. Remember most of the original Hebrews didn't believe Yahweh in ancient times. We must awake out of our sleep. Some will say, "God does not perform evil acts", I agree. But Lucifer visits God sometimes and God asks him

"Have you tired my servant?" Job 1:8. God wants to **see** who really loves him.

Rise O Israel, You have been asleep for too long!

The Apostle Paul was *sincere* in persecuting the gospel, as well as he afterwards was in preaching that faith, he once destroyed. For he thought with himself (Acts 26:9), that he ought, in conscience, for the glory of God, and the advancement of this religious faith, to do many things contrary to the name of the Savior/Yahusha presently known "Jesus of Nazareth". And our Lord tells His disciples (John 16:2), that the time was coming, that whoever killed them would think that he did God's service. God's grace indeed take sincerity as a distinct grace of the Spirit of God and it belongs to sanctification and not to justification, though it seems rather to be what runs through every other grace, than to be distinct from them and is what makes our faith unfeigned, our love without dissimulation. Sanctification [being a Christian] is a gradual and progressive work; it is ***signified*** (2 Pet. 3:18), by a growing in grace and *in* the knowledge of Yahushua/Jesus and it is a work that is; but begun, yet is **not yet finished** and is carried on by ***degrees** (Heb 3:12)*.

Justification is done "simul et semel", it is a complete act at once; it is expressed (Col. 2:10), by the saints being complete in Christ and perfected by his one sacrifice, not by our own righteousness. If the whole work of sanctification, is not our justifying righteousness before God, then certainly the "to credere", or ***act of believing***, which is only a *part* of this work, cannot be it. There are indeed some scriptures listed in these biblical writings, which are by some thoughts to favor this notion, as when it is said in verse 3 of the 26th chapter of Acts. Abraham believed God and it was imputed to him for righteousness. To receive this righteousness we must have faith. Now [right now, not tomorrow's], faith, is the **substance** of things *hope for* and the **evidence** of things not seen Hebrews 11:1. Nevertheless, faith must be allowed to have a very great concern in the business of justification. Hence we are said to be justified by faith (Rom. 5:1), not by faith either as a work performed by us or grace wrought in us, but we are justified by it relatively or objectively, as it respects, apprehends and lays hold on Christ and his righteousness for justification; or we are justified by it organically, as it is a recipient of this blessing, for **faith** is the **hand which receives** the blessing from the Lord and righteousness from the God of our salvation. Not our righteousness, but God's righteousness. It is that grace by which my soul *puts on* Christ's righteousness as a garment (remembering a garment also can be taken off by unbelief) and rejoices therein, by which all boasting in a man's righteousness is *avoided and dead.* There is nothing we can do to earn it, we have to except it [Jesus' righteousness] and say Lord I thank you, knowing how we got it and what it takes to keep it.

Then if Yahweh makes us righteous for free, shouldn't we forgive others freely too? I know I can't always measure up, so I'll come before God in my failures, humbling myself and say father help me by cleansing me, thanking him for answering my petition "**Create in me a *steadfast* spirit**". For in the same way that Adam's sin became ours, the same way the righteousness of Christ becomes ours; or the same way we are made sinners by the disobedience of Adam, we are made righteous by the obedience of Christ (Rom. 5:19). When we "**We confess our sins,** [God] is faithful and just and will forgive us our sins and purify us from all unrighteousness" (1 John 1:9). When we seek forgiveness, the God we serve is quick to "blot out your transgressions for [His] own sake; And [He] will not remember your sins" (Isaiah 43:25). Remember what I told you about King David, well Yahweh said, **"This is a man after my own heart"**. Can you see it? He was forgiven and cleaned for his act. When we need mercy, we can come *boldly* to the throne of grace, that we may obtain mercy and find grace to help in time of need *(Hebrews 4:16).* So when you here someone boasts on their spirituality with God, the words of his or her mouth will identify them. When you hear people begging Yahweh, they truly don't know God's grace. "**Come boldy and now plead your case,** knowing I [Yahweh] wants all the good things for you"!

We did not earn it, but God's words say it and He cannot lie. Therefore, we are *not beggars, or a takers,* as some men have said we

✦ THE EARTH ✦

are, but we ask our Father for any and all things. If He insults us and says harsh things, "He is God; Most Holy and almighty God" we should accept those offensive words, even when we may not feel like hearing those harsh words. Remember, what **feelings** have to do with *believing* Yahweh? My faith doesn't *rest* on my *feelings*; it rest on the **words of God**.

I know He will not harm me; because I respect and trust Him. If Yahweh decides to chastise me; He is almighty, awesome in power; so who can stop Him? Then again, who is more **merciful** than God? He forgave a murderer and called him "A man after my own heart." So, in knowing this, I will *endure* the almighty hand of my God. Yahweh might ask me, "Are you on my side?" I'll happily reply, "Yes Lord; I'm on your side, so reach out your hands and I'll hold on". Will you seek God? Remember the Hebrews in the wilderness complained and what happened to them? **It is impossible to please God**, if you don't *believe* him. **Hebrews 11:6**

I share these truths, because I once totally turned my back on the only living God. I refused to listen to Him and stopped believing in Him. I left His presence and returned to the world. God wouldn't stand for this act of defiance. God was so angry; He took my career; including my finances, my home, health, peace and finally my family. I say this because I don't want you to miss this truth or suffer the troubles I've endured. If God has placed a **calling** on your life, He is not going to let you go. He will come against family, friends, employers; any or everything you touch will be cursed. In doing so, He will be teaching you; "**You are my child**" and I love you enough to correct you! Afterward, all you can do is give up and say; here I am Lord, I see that you love me and will not let me go. I surrender, I'm not my own, I belong to you! I can't fight against you; you are too powerful! Remember God's words, "I will chastise those **I love**". Those same words [God loves me]; I finally remembered and with that remembrance, I gave up on my defiance, because I finally realized I couldn't stand against God. God is almighty, great in power, undefeatable and He will not stop, nor sleep, until He gets what He wants. I remembered God truly loves me and that was enough for me to feel good in a bad situation. This is why I'm writing this book today, because as God loves you and I truly love you too, because my Master, Father, Lord and dear friend loved you first and commanded me to do the same. Every act I see my Father doing or have done, I do my best to **emulate** Him.

CHAPTER 12

WISDOM AND POWER

There is a way to receive the divine wisdom from our Creator. Psalms 4: 5 "Get wisdom, get understanding: forget it not; nether **decline** from the words of my mouth". Psalms 4:7 states "Wisdom is the principle thing: Therefore, get wisdom; and with all your getting, get understanding". Verse 8. "**Exalt her** and she shall **promote** you, she will bring unto thee **honor**, *when* thou embrace her". Jesus said, "You shall not live by bread alone, but *every word* that proceed out of the mouth of God" Matt. 4:4. His words are our spiritual food that we should consume them everyday, sometimes *more* than three times a day. These instructions are not just to ministers, but to all of Yahweh's people. This act of dedication is not happening today (daily feeding; by reading God's word), so without this spiritual diet the church have grown weak.

Jesus could **not perform** *any* **miracles** in Nazareth except for healing a few sick people. The people of Nazareth were apparently plagued by *unbelief* and paid little attention to the claims of Jesus. Mark 6:4-5 Unbelief is a faith killer, faith is not hope and hope is not faith. Now (right now) faith is the evidence, if Yahweh said it, then I believe it, no matter how I feel or *what I see*. This is right now faith; after asking; knowing I already have it; I'm just waiting on the *manifestation* of my hope. While I'm waiting for the manifestation, I'm thanking God for giving whatever I ask for. How do I know this? "Then I said, "Behold, I come; In the scroll of the book it is written of me" Psalms 40:7. Then, I said, 'Here I am—it is written about me in the scroll—I have come to do your will, my God." Hebrew 10:7, 9,23. Everything in His Holy Book is true, there are no metaphors on the faith issue. The bible says what it means and means what it says. Scholars and spiritually dead theologians have lied to you; by theorizing God's word.

Here is more proof of who was who:

Jesus/Yahushua's disciples were mostly *unlearned men*; as to being intellectuals or scholars, but they were wise in knowing the truth of Yahweh Acts 4:13. These scholars and theologians that heard these Apostles marveled and they realized that these men had walked with Yahushua/Jesus. "How could they know so much about things it took us years to learn? I came from the university of Sanctified and study hard for years and I hear things they should not know", maybe were these scholars thoughts. These Apostles performed wonders, healing the sick, casting out demons, all in the name of God. "Hey the University didn't teach me how to do that", I can imagine one might have said. These wonders weren't performed by their own power, but that power that is given from above.

I know you don't hear much about this authority that is given to all believers in our Churches today. Some of the most famous intellectuals and scholars have had trouble receiving this insight and have *theorized* Yahweh's holy words, making them [WORDS] ineffective in creating power, strengthening and producing faith. 1 Corinthians 2:4 and Mark 11:19-21.

The body [members] of the church hasn't read enough of Yahweh's words [Spiritual food]; thereby the church has grown into being a social club. 1 Corinthians 2 states, "And I, brethren, when I came to you, came not with excellence of speech or of wisdom, declaring unto you the testimony of God. v2. For I determined not to know any thing among you, save Jesus and him crucified. (The Cross and blood sacrifice) v3. I was with you in weakness,

✦ THE EARTH ✦

in fear and much trembling. v4. My speech and my preaching was *not* with enticing words of **man's wisdom,** but in **demonstration** of the *Spirit and Power.*" This verse shouldn't have been separated from the preceding verse 4 and it concludes; that your **faith** should *not stand* in the wisdom of men, but your faith only standing in the **power** of God. Power is the *stability* of our faith. What is this Power Yahweh's servant Paul talking about? Those miracles that were performed, were performed only by the authority in the name of Jesus. This act of using Jesus' authority includes literally calling upon his name. Paul was saying that he has received these gifts too, delivered and controlled by the Holy Spirit.

This is not our power, it is given by God and we did not earn it. He said in Matt. 10:7-8 "As you go, *proclaim* (A black secular artist emphasized this proclamation effectively, "**Say it loud . . . .**"). You know the rest of it and it have nothing to do with Godliness, but only pride and we know pride causes destruction Psalms 16:18. This message: 'The kingdom of heaven has come near, includes Yahweh's servants telling His people "loudly". v8.'Heal the sick, raise the dead, cleanse those who have leprosy, drive out demons. Freely you have received; freely give. This power does not operate at our will; it operates only as the Spirit of God moves by Faith 1 Cor.12:6-11. After standing on your regular faith; in times of need this Gift takes over; it takes control, giving us the "All thing are possible Faith". Theologians say those acts are done away with, so this is my point; *they shouldn't be.*

But you will receive power when the Holy Spirit comes on you and you will be my witnesses in Jerusalem, and in all Judea and Samaria and to the ends of the earth" Acts 1:8. If you don't go to church, look at what you are missing! I say this because Yahweh tell you to study and know His words, treasure wisdom as fine gold, by doing so; you will receive spiritual food, guidance, and finally, Power (Act 1:8). Remember I said receive and I didn't say we've earn it or deserve it, this manifestation is given freely. The book of Acts speaks of the miracles performed by Jesus' disciples. I contend God have **not changed**, the church has changed. We must believe, before we can receive. Remember, I've said once I lost my health because of my defiance? Well, I should have died, but my God had mercy on me and I recovered. Hear Yahweh words, let it [God's Words] be the **apple of your eye**, thereby; writing them in your heart. Meditate on them [speaking orally]; thereby printing them on the tablets of your heart and keeping them in your mist. Feed yourself with the spiritual words of Jesus. "Faith comes by hearing and hearing by the *Word* of God" Rom 10:17. We need to keep God's Word in our midst, reading and hearing them over and over and over. Like in ancient times, as well as today, man considered this was too much work to do, (over-over-over-over-over), but this is God's way. He deserves the **most dedication** or as Yahweh sees it *"sacrifice"*. Yahweh **lives** in the mist of praises; fasting, studying and I'll give Him my time, not just by studying and going to church, but bringing my church (the Holy Spirit inside of me) to the church that I attend.

Let Yahweh's spiritual words live in you. When we diligently feed on His words, a spiritual explosion is just waiting to happen. This is the difference in a spiritually active church and a dead one. This explosion might not happen each and everyday, but if it never happens, then the church is dead. You might be the one to bring it back to life. Will these *dead bones live*? **Ezekiel 37:3. v4** Then, *prophesy* to those dry bones "**Hear the words of God**". When this act of sacrifice becomes sweet to you (you start enjoying doing *it* over, and over and over) in praises, readings, fasting and much prayer, that is when you are entering to the receiving part; empowerment is coming! Yahweh is alive, but in some churches today, He is just a figure in a story. Peter said, why marvel at this as *if* I've done it myself? **Acts 3:12.**

The spirit of God produces something supernatural. Not just an ordinary emotional event, but is something fantastic and amazing. Some people say, "It just emotions", but I want you to see how your devoted ancestors acted; blowing their horns, trumpets, dancing and making loud praises to Yahweh. King David got so excited that he danced out his clothes (not completely naked) 2 Samue16:14. It is not just emotional; *it's spiritual.* I can see the proudness of people thinking more of them than they should. As with Michal, King David's wife not understanding her husband's motive and thinking he had lowered himself before the people, reproached him bitterly, and despised him in her heart. But David's motive for rejoicing was pure. When the words of God come **alive** in you, sometimes you will have church alone; **all by yourself.** The fire of God's anointing will start burning and you have to give God what He loves; sincere praise and worship Psalms 22:3. If your church doesn't do this, you can do it at home before you get there and then watch what a difference it makes once you get to church. You might be the one that brings life back to God's temple. All mankind have ears and eyes, but not a spiritual ear and eye **Matt. 11:15, 13:9.** "That is emotional foolishness", one might think that reads this.

A wise man once said, "You can't **stay** warm, unless you stay **close** to the **fire.** Then get close to God, all that hear. Yahweh says it, "He that has an ear, let him hear." Matthew 11:15. God's faith filled spoken word is just as effective, as when He walked this earth, as God would say the very words Himself. We must learn to speak the life producing Words and spiritually do the things Jesus did on this earth. "The things that I do, you shall do also, and greater things shall you do, because I go to my Father" John 14:12. Jesus gives us all "Authority", John 14:17 "Even the Spirit of truth, whom the world cannot receive because it see Him not, neither know Him; but **you know Him**; for He dwell with you, and shall be in you [Holy Spirit].

CHAPTER 13

A New Commandment

God loves all mankind, he doesn't care where you come from or what economical class you live in or any of those things. God's commandment is to love him and all mankind. 1 Peter 4:8 "Above all", *love* each other deeply, because **love covers** over a multitude of sins. In John 13:34. Our Savior said, "A new command I give you; *Love* one another. As I have loved you, so you must love one another." I'm a retired soldier and whatever I was ordered to do, I've found myself doing it. I'm a servant of Yahweh and whatever he tells me to do, "I'm determined to do it". John 14:16 "By this everyone will **know** that you are my disciples, if you love one another, and this new command will fulfill all of the commandments of the Law of Moses. Jesus didn't water the commandments down or make them easy; Jesus fulfilled every requirement of the Law by his atonement. He told us, if we walk in his love; we will fulfill all of the requirements of the commandments. One may say, "When a man hates me, I have the *right* to hate him back." Remember, godly **love is not a feeling**; it is an **act or a reaction**. It does not matter if man act toward you is positive or negative; Yahweh tells you to love. 1 Corinthians 13:4 states, "Love is patient, love is kind. It does not envy, it does not boast, it is not proud". One may ask,

✦ The Earth ✦

"How can I do this?" The one and only true answer; make it God's responsibility by asking Him, "Create in me a *clean heart* that I will not sin against you." Afterward, we should live our lives yielding to Yahweh's spiritual operation. We should make life about our relationship with God, instead of letting our feelings be in offense [hurt], because of man's unpleasing actions toward us.

Psalms 51:10 says it this way, "Create in me a pure heart, O God and renew a steadfast spirit within me." Yahweh says in John 16:23, "In that day you will no longer ask me anything. Very truly I tell you, my father will give you whatever you ask in my name." This means that you don't have to ask verbally all of the time, sometimes you can just imagine it, because you might be angry at someone at the time and you need Yahweh's help right away, because you are maybe hot and your anger is burning. Just want it, whatever you are requesting from God, desperately.

Create in me, Oh Lord; I need it right now, that I will not *sin against you*. You (Yahweh) are almighty, I can't have you mad with me too, so cool and take away this anger in me. "I can handle man in his anger, but I can do nothing with You (Yahweh), I can't protect myself against You, You are almighty, no where can I run or hide, so I'll *quickly humble* myself to Your almighty presence (I've seen your Power). "You own me and nowhere can I hide from You", see yourself in or with this spirit.

John 14:17 states "The Spirit of truth. The "world" **cannot accept Him**, because it neither sees Him nor knows Him. But you know Him, for He lives with you and will be in you. When you read God's words over and over again continuously, these living words will *start living* **in you**. We need the Love to come alive in us. Love envies not, love is not puffed up; it endures all, it believe all, it suffers all and rejoice in it 1 Corinthians 13:3-8.

"Man, you have to be out of your mind!" some might think. **Yes I am out of my mind,** I rather live with the mind of God, rather than with my own mind.

I remember where my mind took me; it took me to a defiant spiritual place and I remember Yahweh's chastisement. This is why

I can honestly say; "I need you Lord, each and everyday". I pray that you receive this truth with no offense and may you have received the spirit of truth, because offense that is not my intent. If you are offended by this, then you really don't want Yahweh's instructions and blessings. But if something on the inside of you starts desiring to know more, it is Yahweh calling you, He is coming *alive* **in** *you*. This is why scholars today don't know how to teach God's words, this wisdom is spiritually revealed and received.

Remember the thief that died on the cross with Jesus and he was told by our Saviour; **"You will be with me in paradise"**? Well this thief never did anything godly, he wasn't baptized, he didn't sit on the morning bench until he was filled with the Holy Spirit or he didn't say three Hail Marys or any other supposed spiritual ritual. He met love reincarnated in the flesh and saw **he needed love** and he was accepted by love. I'm not professing men can live all of their lives; knowing death is coming near and repent at the last minute and God will accept them, nor, am I professing this could not happen. God knows the thoughts and the intent of all men's hearts. This is Yahweh's business and He knows it better than I do. Personally; I wouldn't want to take that risk, because it took years after backsliding from God, for Him to anoint me again with His spirit and power. There is only one *Love* doctrine, whatever way you get to agape love, is Yahweh's doctrine. Yahweh's words say, "draw near to me and I come near you" James 4:8, I'll teach you all things John 14:26. In this life process, you don't get holy over night; it's a process Hebrew 10:23, 35. If you are in the wrong church, God will show you the way; just keep on loving as God commanded. That is the key to Heaven Door.

If another minister doesn't agree with my view, I say, whatever way you get the church to Yahweh by love is a way heaven too. "By this [love, agape], **men will *know*** you are my disciples". If it is any spiritual doctrine doesn't make love the **main issue**, I would tell people to run, not walk from that ministry. In love there can be no hate, no envy, no pride and no stealing or any other sin. If I break God's covenant and sin, I have an advocate [Jesus], in whom upon repentance, cleans me again. Man need to see this simple truth. Each individual eat food every day, but your spiritual man is staving, he is nearly dead. My desire for you is to let Him [Holy Spirit] come to life in you. I'm not just talking about Acts 2:38, this is just the beginning of spiritual maturity; I want the Holy Spirit to take control of you; with all of its benefits available to you. We need to know not just the good words of Yahweh, but all His teachings, including the hard to except words and so by feeding on the word, growing in word; the difficult [spiritual] revelations will start to reveal themselves to you.

CHAPTER 14

YAHWEH's Name Has Power

1 John.2:1 "MY little children, these things I write unto you, that ye sin not. And if any man sin, we have an **advocate** with the Father, Jesus his Son "the righteous" This is where we receive our righteousness. I love the name of Jesus. I was converted to Christianity in under this name (Jesus). God's true name is **Yah**. King James bible in Psalms 68:4 states God name is Jah. The letter J started existing in writings about 400 years ago, it did not exist during recorded biblical time. Check the historical facts. Therefore Jah; is really saying "Yah" as in "Hallelu-**jah**" meaning "**praise-Yah**". This is why I use **Yahushua**; "Yah's Son" for and with the name of Jesus in this book. The sound of our Savior name have been lost to us, either mistakenly or intentionally to exclude our biblical black lineage from the history books. Christians have been taught "There is power in the name of our God", then why not call him by his true name? The sound of Jesus' name comes from his Father; who is named, "Yah" Psalms 68:4. Therefore I will use the sound and meaning of God's true name and apply it to His Son. Yah-meaning-God as we presently know it and **hoo-shoo'-ah**—meaning—Son of God. The son that we know as Jesus. Therefore it sound like this; Ya-hoo-shoo'-ah, the same sound as in *Joshua* [whose true name was Hoshe'a] in the bible. Some might ask why this is important to know. (1) God's true name and biblical ethnicity is important to those of us who are charged with the responsibility of preaching the living words of Yahweh Acts 20:27; Timothy 4:2.

The true name of Yahweh is also supported by historical data; Josiah was really called Yoshiyahu in Hebrew and means "healed by Yah" or "supported of Yah". Yoshiyahu was the King of Judah (*641-609 BC*). (2) Biblical identification and ethnicity is important to those of us who have been charged with the responsibility of Evangelism **2 Timothy 4:5** and to the Apologetics ("**Defending the Faith**", **1 Peter 3:15; Jude 1:3**). (3) Identification and biblical ethnicity is important to those of us who are charged with the task of Christian education **Matt.:28:16-20**) "Baptizing them in the **name** of the Father; Son and Holy Ghost" and "Teach them to observe **all** things whatsoever I have commanded you". (4) Biblical ethnicity is important in the realm of race relations. The primary source for these conclusions is drawn from the bible and recorded history.

We accept what Yahushua did on the cross and profess with our mouth what Yahweh's son did and believe that when Yahushua rose from the grave and was literally brought back dead men to life that were in their graves. He completed the Hebrew ritual by ascending to Heaven and going into the most "Holy of Holies" and there Yahushua covered the mercy seat with His perfect blood for the sins of all mankind". The cost of the cruses for mankind's sin was **paid in full**. Our sins are no longer just covered as the Old Testament blood sacrifice did, but we are **cleansed** from our sins. This was the final act in atoning for our sins with blood sacrifices. Yahushua interceded for us, "Give them whatever they ask Father". "As obedient children, do not conform to the evil desires you had when you lived in ignorance" 1 Pet.1:14-17.

CHAPTER 15

IDENTIFYING THE TRUTH

The sons of Judah were Perez, **Hezron**, *Carmi, Hur, and* **Shobal**. *1 Chronicles 4:1-43.*

Shobab is a very similar name of a different individual listed in 1 Chronicles 2:18 "And Caleb the son of Hezron (The brother of Shobal) begat children of Azubah his wife and of Jerioth: her sons are these; Jesher, and **Shobab** and Ardon. Custom continued in the Hebrew tribe of Judah, by Caleb naming his son "Shobab" and that name continued with King David naming his son Shobab (See how the name pattern continued, "A son named after a relative?).

Caleb sometimes transliterated Kaleb; is a figure who appears in the bible as a representative of Judah. Caleb the Son of Jephunneh." He was the first to speak up and say, **"Let us go and conquer this land"** (paraphrased). Caleb, who encouraged Israel to follow God in spite of the opposition from the other 10 spies. Only two came back with a good report, Joshua (his real name was Hoshe'a) was the son of Nun was the other to give a godly report. Joshua was from the tribe of Ephraim [Joseph half Egyptian son]. **Rahab,** who was an ancestor to King David hid the two spies that Joshua sent to spy out the land, and this would have been impossible unless they were of the same racial color and we know Rahab was a Black woman by being a Hitite. Caleb's father was called a Kenizzite (Numbers 32:12, Joshua 14:6,14) and the Kenizzites are listed (Genesis 15:19) [blacks] as one of the nations who lived in the land of Canaan at the time that God made a covenant with Abram (Abraham) to give that land to his descendants forever (Genesis 17:8). One of the sons of Caleb was Jephunneh, who bore Iru, Elah, and Naam. The son of Elah was Kenaz. 1 Chronicles 4:16. The sons of Jehallelel were Ziph, Ziphah, Tiria and Asarel.

1 Chronicles 4:17 The sons of **Ezrah (1)**: Jether, **Mered**, Epher and Jalon. One of Mered's wives gave birth to **Miriam**, Shammai and Ishbah the father of Eshtemoa. Mered is a biblical character who was from the Tribe of Judah and was the husband of **Bithiah**, daughter of Pharaoh of Eygpt. **Bithiah** was the foster mother of *Moses*. Maybe one reason she adopted Moses was because of her husband's influence because his Hebrew bloodline. I want to reveal the truth in the following verse; **1 Chronicles 4:18** "His wife from the tribe of Judah gave birth to Jered the father of Gedor, Heber the father of Soko and Jekuthiel the father of Zanoah. These were the children of Pharaoh's daughter Bithiah, whom Mered had married." We know Bithiah was an **Egyptian** and could not have been from the tribe of Judah; but she was called the mother of those children. The reason for this was the same as Shem accepting all of Eber sons as **his own** and Terah acceptance of Sarah, the first wife of Abraham as his daughter. Jacob/Israel accepted Joseph's two sons as his own. This was the same customary method of the non-biological children being called their children, when they were not biologically. Sarah was not Terah's daughter, nor Abram sister; she was Abram's brother, Haran's daughter.

Kish; son of Abd and Azariah son of the Levite, Jehallelel is mentioned in 2 Chronicles 29:11; "My sons, be not now negligent: for the LORD **has chosen** you to stand before Him, to **serve Him**, and that you should minister to Him and burn incense". The incense that we burn before God today is our "Praises", so fill your room with this great smell by loudly proclaiming .... "Thou God is

Holy and worthy to be praised!" 2 Chronicles 29:12. These Levites that was set to work: The Kohathites, Mahath son of Amasai and Joel son of Azariah. Those chosen from the Merarites were Kish son of Abdi and Azariah son of Jehallelel, and from the *Gershonites*, Joah son of Zimmah and Eden son of Joah.

Eshtemoa is a descendant of **Bithiah**, princess of Egypt and her husband Mered and this name was later the name of a **town** in the mountains of Judah, which was allotted land to the priests. (Jos 15:50) EZRA 9:1 states, "The people of Israel and the priests, and the Levites, have not **separated** themselves from the people of the lands, doing according to their abominations, even of the Canaanites, the Hittites, the Perizzites, the Jebusites, the Ammonites, the Moabites, the Egyptians and the Amorites." Our Black ministers have mostly preached biblical facts only from the Holy Bible, in which I was trained. Most of them preach biblical doctrine, lacking emphasis on biblical history. So where were the Black Scholars and Historians and Theologians? These historians and scholars have no excuse and most of them [**intelligentsia**] argue about these recorded facts. This makes even the lay people scratch their heads and ask; "Where is the wisdom of God?" Historical data is *revealing* this truth that has been *hid* for years. This is why I'm revealing this truth in detail, name by name, family by family, tribe by tribe and clan by clan. I contend that you should know this history because God says, "My people are destroyed because of the lack of spiritual knowledge "**Hosea 4:6**

Joshua's father was named Nun in the Hebrew Bible, and he was a man from the tribe of **Ephraim**, grandson of Ammihud, the son of Elishama, **(1 Chronicles 7:26-27)** He grew up in and may have lived most of his life in the Israelites' Egyptian captivity. Joshua was Israel's leader after Moses. Ephraim was the son of Joseph, and he was Joshua ancestor.

Ammihud was the father of the Ephraimite's *chief* **Elishama** at the time of the Exodus **(Book of Numbers 1:10; 2:18; 7:48, 53)**. The father of Talmai, king of Geshur whom **Absalom** (King David son) fled after the murder of Amnon **(2 Samuel 13:37)**. He was the son of Omri and the father of Uthai (1 Chronicles 9:4). Prophet Samuel also was an Ephrathite.

Levi was the third son of Jacob and Leah. He fathered three sons; Gershon, Kohath and Merari. A similar genealogy is given in the Book of Exodus where it is added that among Kohath's sons was *Amram*, who married a woman named Jochebed. Jochebed was closely related to Amram's father and they were the biological parents of **Moses, Aaron, and Miriam,** who were leaders of the Israelite tribe of Levi. Ezekiel, Ezra and Malachi were all levites. All of these people had Ham's genes; who is known the father of the Black race.

Gershon according to the Torah, Gershon was the eldest of the sons of *Levi* and the patriarchal founder of the Gershonites, one of the four main divisions among the Levites in biblical times. The Gershonites were charged with the care of the outer tabernacle including components such as the tent and its covering, screens, doors, and hangings.

Kohath was one of the sons of Levi and the patriarchal founder of the **Kohathites**, one of the four **main** divisions of the Levites in biblical times. In some apocryphal texts, such as the testament of Levi and the Book of Jubilees, Levi's wife, who was Kohath's mother, was named Milkah/Mekah in the list above; a daughter of Aram, of the **seeds** of the **sons** of Terah.

Merari was one of the sons of Levi, he was the patriarchal founder of the Merarites, one of the four main divisions among the Levites in biblical times; the Hebrew word Merari means *sad bitter*. The Merarites were charged with the care of the boards of the tabernacle and related items, as well as the pillars of the court all around and related components.

Jochebed was a daughter of Levi and mother of Aaron, Miriam and Moses. She was the *wife* of **Amram**, as well as his aunt. She lived in Egypt where the descendants of Israel were being oppressed. The Targum Pseudo-Jonathan identifies Jochebed as also having been wife of Elitzaphon Ben Parnach and the mother of **Eldad and Medad**; whom Joshua asked Moses to forbid from prophecy, but

Moses argued that it was a good thing that others could prophesy and that ideally all the Israelites would prophesy.

Amram was the son of Gershon and the father of Aaron, Moses, Miriam and the husband of Jochebed. Naturally if Moses live in the King of Egypt house for 40 years passing as the king's grandson, also proves Moses was a man of color, as well as his parents.

Moses' mother Jochebed was also his Great Aunt; meaning she was his father's Aunt too. Moses mother and father was of the one gene, mixed Cushite. So this Black gene came for one or possibly both of his grand parents; which was Gershon; who married to an unmentioned wife (She was from his distant kinsmen, the Egyptians). Gerson's parents were Milcah and Levi and both had Cushite genes. Levi's and wife parent, grand-parents had a Cushite gene Peleg; son of Eber and grandson of Nimrod.

Simeon was the son of Jacob/Israel. 1 Chon 1:24 states, "The sons of Simeon were Nemuel, Jamin, Jarib, Zerah and Shaul, the sons of the Canaanite woman, wife of Simeon. Although some classical rabbinical sources argue that the mother of his children and his wife was ***Bonah***; one of the women from Shechem [Canaanite city]. While other classical rabbinical sources argue that Simeon's wife and the mother of his children was Dinah, who was his sister. Simeon and his sister Dinah were atleast distant Cushites. One of the cities they dwelt in was called **Beersheba**.

Shaul; Saul was the first king of Israel (1021-1000 BC). All that is known of Saul; the Benjamite comes from the biblical books of Samuel I and Samuel II. He was anointed king by the prophet Samuel as a concession to popular pressure, after delivering the town of Jabesh-Gilead from Ammonite oppression. Samuel's rejection of Saul and Saul's jealousy of David led to Saul's decline. He died battling the Philistines at Mount Gilboa; David delivered the Israelites and paid tribute to his fallen King. Saul was the son of **Kish** of the family of the Matrites and a member of the tribe of Benjamin, one of the twelve Tribes of Israel. 1 Samuel 9:1-2; 10:21; 14:51; Acts 13:21

Saul married Ahinoam, daughter of Ahimaaz. They had four sons and two daughters. Saul sons were Jonathan, Abinadab, Malchishua and Ish-bosheh. His daughters were named Merab and Michal. Saul also had a concubine named Rizpah, daughter of Aiah, who bore him two sons; Armoni and Mephibosheth. (2 Samuel 21:8) Saul offered Merab to David as a wife after his victory over Goliath, but David didn't seem to have been interested in the arrangement. (1 Samuel 18:17-19) Saul then gave his other daughter Michal in marriage to David (1 Samuel 18:20-27), but when David became Saul's rival to the kingship, Saul gave Michal in marriage to Palti, son of Laish (1 Samuel 25:44). Three of Saul's sons; Jonathan, Abinadab and Malchishua died with him at Mount Gilboa (1 Samuel 31:2; Chronicles 10:2). Ish-bosheth became king of Israel at the age of forty. (2 Samuel 2:10) Michal was returned as wife to David.

Ahinoam was Saul wife; who was a daughter of Ahimaaz. She bore four sons and two daughters, one of whom is **Michal**, David's first wife (King David son received Ham's Black genes from both parents). A woman from Jezreel, who became David's first acknowledged wife, after he fled from Saul and left Michal, his first-ever wife and the mother of his son Amnon behind. Amnon was David's first-born son.

David additional wives were Zeruiah and Abigail. Abigail's father was Nahash and they were also David's biological sisters by his mother, David father was Jesse, but he was not his sisters' father.

Ish-bosheth, son of King Saul, reigned for two years and was killed by two of his own captains. **(2 Samuel 4:5)** The only male descendant of Saul to survive was **Mephibosheth**; Jonathan's son, (2 Samuel 4:4) who was five years old when his father and grandfather Saul had died in battle. In time, he came under the protection of King David, because of David love for his father Jonathan. (2 Samuel 9:7-13) Mephibosheth had a young son, Micah, (2 Samuel 9:12) of whom nothing more is heard. Armoni and Mephibosheth, who were Saul's sons with his concubine, Rizpah were given by

David along with the five sons of Merab Saul's daughter to the Gibeonites, who killed all of them. (2 Samuel 21:8-9) Michal was childless. (2 Samuel 6:23).

Ahimaaz was a mixed Canaanite, and son and successor of Zadok in the office of *High Priest* **(1 Chronicles 6:8, 53)**. He was swift of foot and was the first to carry to David tidings of the defeat of Absalom, although he refrained from delicacy of feeling, from telling him of his death **(**2 Sam. 18:19-33). He may have been the same Ahimaaz who took as wife *Basemath*, one of Solomon's daughters (I Kings 4:15). Subsequent king of Israel, Ahaz also married daughters of the high priest.

Zadok (meaning "Righteous") was a priest descended from Eleazar the son of Aaron, brother of Moses. He aided King David during the revolt of his son Absalom and was consequently instrumental in bringing King Solomon to the throne. After Solomon's building of the first Temple in Jerusalem, Zadok was the first High Priest to serve there. The prophet **Ezekiel** extols the sons of Zadok as staunch opponents of paganism during the era of its pagan worship and indicates their birthright to unique duties and privileges in the future temple (Ezekiel 42:13, 43:19). Zadok, The son of Ahitub, son of Amaryah, son of Azaryah, son of Mirayoth, son of Zerachyah, son of Uzzi, son of Bukki, son of Avishua, son of *Phineas*—Ezra 7:1-4

Eleazar: His wife was the daugther of *Putiel*, who bore him Phinehas. Putiel' name derises from "Phut or Put", who was a son of Ham and proves **Putiel** was a descendant of **Put. Exodus 6:25**. Both parents of Phinehas had Black genes.

Machir was the son of Manasseh and father of **Gilead** Number 26:29. Manasseh was the son of Joseph and the Egyptian woman. In the Torah's account of the journey of the Israelites after the Exodus, Machir is portrayed as **conquering** the territories known as Gilead and Bashan, which had previously been occupied by Amorites. Machir's descendants are described as having settled in Gilead and Bashan and consequently is a key figure in Gilead's history. The Isaric Jews of **Indonesia** claim descent from Machir.

✦ The Earth ✦

According to the Books of Samuel, Machir son of Amiel was the name of a descendant of the Machir mentioned above and resided at Lo-Debar. Biblical historical text states that here he looked after **Meribaal**, the son of **Jonathan**, until David took over his care, and he also looked after David himself, when David found himself a fugitive.

Nehemiah was Governor of Judah; meaning he was from the tribe of Judah. Neh. 11:4 "Of the children of *Judah*; Athaiah the son of Uzziah, the son of Zechariah, the son of Amariah, the son of Shephatiah, the son of Mahalaleel of the children of Perez." All the names listed in this Chapter of Nehemiah had Ham's genes (Cushite).

Isaiah was a prophet who lived in the 8th-century BC Kingdom of Judah. The first verse of the Book of Isaiah states that he prophesied during the reigns of Uzziah (or Azariah), Jotham, Ahaz, and Hezekiah, all were kings of Judah. All of Judah descendants had Ham's black genes.

Jeremiah was a prophet, son of Hilkiah of the priests. He was the grandson of Zadok and the same individual that stated, "Sons of Zion who vistage [face] is like **coal**." This wasn't a symbolic statement, coal is **very dark** black.

Hosea was a prophet from the tribe of Ephraim, half Egyptian, as well as the prophet **Amos**.

Joel was a prophet from the trible of **Judah**, as well as the prophet **Micah** and the prophet **Haggi**.

Obadiah was a prophet, said to have been a convert to Judaism from Edom and his Canaanite wife, a descendant of Eliphaz; son of Esau, who was a friend of righteous Job.

Nahum was a prophet from the tribe of Judah (brother of Modiah or Hodiah) Chron 4:19.

Zephaniah was the son of Cushi, who was a prophet and his father's name alone identifies his ethnicity, descendant of **Cush**, the son of Ham.

Zechariah was a prophet from the tribe of Levi. Jesus is quoted as stating that Zechariah son of Barachiah was **killed** between the altar and the temple.

By having this biblical knowledge, I know how sensitive and emotional people can get over religious issues. I write this book to encourage and do it as God directs me too. Thereby, I know everyone will not receive God's message and some will be offended by it contents. I make no apologies for any offense taken, because offense is not intended.

In the Book of **Malachi,** Targum Jonathan, an Aramaic paraphrase adds after the name of Malachi, "Cujus nomen appelatur Ezra scriba," whose name is called Ezra the Scribe, thus claiming that the great and good **Ezra** is Malachi, who was a priest and from the tribe of Levi. Almost every prophetic book in the Old Testament was written by men of color; who had the genes [one drop] that America once would consider as "Black People." Currently today in some dictionaries, this definition is still present.

Manasseh was the first son of **Joseph** and **Asenath;** the Egyptians. (**Genesis 41:50-52**). Jacob also blessed Ephraim over his older brother. (**Genesis 48:20**) "Manasseh" in Hebrew means "forgetful." Asenath was an Egyptian [Black] woman whom Pharaoh gave to Joseph as wife and the daughter of Potipherah, a priest of On. (**Genesis 41:50-52**) Manasseh was born in Egypt before the arrival of the children of Israel from Canaan. (Genesis 48:5). Manasseh had a son, Asriel, with his wife, and **Machir** was born to his Aramean concubine. (1 Chronicles 7:14). Manasseh and Ephraim descendant live among each other Joshua 16:9.

Ephraim was according to the Book of Genesis, the second son of Joseph and Asenath. Asenath was an Egyptian woman whom Pharaoh gave to Joseph as wife, and the daughter of Potipherah, a priest of On. (Genesis 41:50-52 Ephraim was born in Egypt before the arrival of the children of Israel from Canaan. (Genesis 48:5). Ephraim had sons: Shuthelah, Beker and Tahan. However, 1 Chronicles 7 claims that he also had two more sons, Ezer and Elead, who were killed by local men who came to rob him of his cattle. He then had another son, Beriah, who carried on his name. (1 Chronicles 7:20-23). The **Samaritans** (a mixture of the tribes of Menasseh, Ephraim and partially Benjamin and Levi), who were people of Samaria. It replaced the title "Children of Israel."

Astriel was the mother of Machir; the son of Manasseh (Joseph's half Egyptian son) and father of Gilead. **Gilead** was the son of **Machir** and hence the grandson of **Manasseh** [half Egyptian] great-grandson of Joseph and greatx4 grandson of Abraham and Sarah. He also may have been the founder of the Israelite tribal group of Gilead. A number of biblical scholars suspect that the distinction of the Joseph tribes (including Benjamin) is that they were the only Israelites which went from Egypt and returned, while the **main** Israelite tribes simply emerged as a subculture from the Canaanites [black] and had remained in Canaan throughout.

Judah (Tribe of Judah) the father of **Perez** and Zerah and their mother was **Tamar**. Perez the father of Hezron, Hezron the father of Ram, Ram the father of Amminadab, Amminadab the father of Nahshon, Nahshon the father of Salmon, Salmon the father of Boaz; whose mother was Rahab. Boaz was the father of Obed; whose mother was Ruth, and father of Jesse. Jesse was the father of King David. David was the father of Solomon, whose mother previously was Uriah, the Hitite's wife.

Micah, who was the daughter of Aram and the father of Uz, Hul, Gether and Mash. Aram and his family lived in all of the land between the Tigris and Euphrates rivers "to the north of the Chaldees to the border of the mountains of Asshur and the land of 'Arara. Genesis 10:11 says the land of Asshur was **Nimrod's land** for his people and he ruled the Chaldeans, who was called "Black Heads".

Uz Genesis 10:23 was a name to an area of ancient **Middle East**, later inhabited by the Old Testament character named Job. **Job 1:1** states, "There was a man in the land of Uz, whose name was Job; perfect and upright and one that feared God." Jeremiah 25:20 notes, "And **all** the mingled people, all the kings of the land of Uz, all the kings of the land of the Philistines and Ashkelon".

By the beginning of the 1st Millennium BCE they had adopted the general Canaanite language of the region. In the course of its history, Uz has been **ruled** by the Canaanites, the Philistines and the Egyptians. All of these bibilical listed nations were descendants of Ham.

Before this time of mixing with other nations, Numbers 11:4 states: "And the mixed multitiude that was among them fell into lusting", desiring the food of Egypt.

The friends of Job "The righteous Cushite" were **Eliphaz**, son of Esau, and his mother was Elon the **Hittite**; a clan from Canaan. **Bildad**, son of Shulah, son of Abraham and Keturah, the **Cushite**. **Zophar**, the Naamathite and the city of Naamah in Canaan was given his name. **Elihu**, a descendant of Buz, son of Nahor and Milcah and all three had Cushite origin.

One can theorize these facts or counter questionable historic facts, but all Christians believe biblical facts and these biblical facts show Black-intermixing occurred in all Hebrew tribes. Biblical facts are the main support of my contentions.

The "one drop of African blood rule" that enslaved America's Blacks reveal scholars and historians evaded biblical truth about this issue [blackness]. These wealthy Caucasian men planned and succeeded, "**I'll change history**" and have these people calling on the name of God's son that **did not exist**." Additionally, see the act our ancestors; "**Give us barabbas!**" Our ancestors requested the release of a thief and crucified Jesus. Now can you see Yahweh's anger toward mankind? So repent, because He is full of mercy. "I didn't do it", some might say. "I'll remember your sins unto your children's generations" Exodus 34:7. He knew what we were going to do to his son, but in the same verse [Exodus 34:7], He states how *merciful* He will be upon repentance. Fleshly man hates the truth most of the time. Can you see who Jesus was talking to when he told them "You are of your Father, **the Devil**" John 8:44-45. This wasn't a biological description, it was a spiritual discription of what Jesus saw in these men. Notice they were "**Ministers of the Gospel**". Jesus saw devils in the church teaching his people and he told them exactly who was their father. God ask all mankind, "Who is your Father?". Remember those insults during childhood, "Who is your daddy?" Now you know not to get mad when people intentionally insult you, because they are revealing who their father really is.

"Yahweh is my father", should have been an answer from those who had no biological father present in their lives. If God is your father, then remind yourself each day and **act accordingly**. Let continue with our biblical ancestors:

Another Milcah, who was the great-grandmother to Aram's daughter Milcah and she was the daughter of Haran and the wife of Nahor in Genesis. Milcah was born to Haran, who had another daughter, **Iscah—[Sarai]**. This Haran was the brother of Abraham and Nahor; who had a son named Lot. (Gen. 11:27,29.) Haran, Abraham's brother, died in Ur before his father Terah. (Gen. 11:28.) (Gen. 11:29). Remember the earlier proof of Cushite ethnicity is in our fore-fathers though Eber's wife and they resided in the *Chaldees*. Although Leviticus would later *outlaw* marriages between aunt and nephew (Lev.18:14; 20:19), it did not rule out marriage between uncle and niece. (See, e.g., Gunther Plaut, The Torah: a Modern Commentary, 881. New York: UAHC, 1981.) Milcah and Nahor had eight children, Uz, Buz, Kemuel, Chesed, Hazo, Pildash, Jidlaph, and **Bethuel**. Bethuel is biblically mentioned as the nephew of Abraham and the father of Laban and Rebekah; mother of Jacob and Esau. (Gen. 22:21). Bethuel lived in Padan-aram and is described as "Aramaean", descendants of **Aram**, son of Shem.

A generation later, Isaac sent Jacob back to Padan-aram to take a wife from among Bethuel's granddaughters, rather than from among the Canaanites. The reason were *not* because Canaanites were Black as some attest, but it was because their spiritual relationship with Yahweh. The Bible gives proof that the Hebrews were of a mixed Black [Cushite] race with King Solomon stating "I'm Black" and the Prophet Jeremiah stating, "The children of Zion face is black as coal." Laban and his family were described as dwelling in Paddan-aram in Mesopotamia. Targum Jonathan says that Providence granted Milcah conception in the merit of her sister Sarah [Sarah was Abraham's sister *only* by Terah accepting Sarah as his own daughter; when his son Haran died, as Israel did with Joseph's two sons. (Targum Jonathan to Gen. 22:20.) Nahor also had four children by his concubine, Reumah. **(Gen. 22:24.)** Milcah's son Bethuel moved to Padan-aram and fathered Rebekah. **(Gen. 22:23; 24:15, 24, 47)**.

It is believed by some scholars, Milcah's granddaughter Rebekah then married the same Milcah nephew Isaac (Gen. 24:67; 25:20) and gave birth to Jacob (Gen. 25:21-26), whose name was later changed to Israel. (Gen. 32:28; 35:10. Now let's go back to Abraham's father Terah, who had to have Ham's genes from **Azurad**, dauther of Nimrod, mother of Peleg and Joktan. The Babylonian Talmud says, "Terah took a wife and her name was *Amsalai* (some Rabbis call her Amtilai), the daughter of **Karnevo** and the wife of Terah conceived and bare him a son in those days." **Jasher 7:50**. This connects her to the *Horite* caste who maintained a shrine as *Karnak* on the Nile. It may also explain why she isn't named in Genesis. Levi's wife was also named Micah and from the ancient customary name pattern, Micah; Levi wife was kin to *all* of the Micah before her without marriage consideration of any of these Micah(s). This information was problematic to the rabbis that Abraham's mother was probably the daughter of a Horite priest. We shouldn't be surprised by this. It is a key trait of the Horite marriage and ascendency pattern that Horite men **only** married the daughters of Horite priests. Milcah (2) or Milka, who was the wife of Levi's lineage is unknown except in The Book of Jubilees. It states, Milka "Of the daughters of Aram, of the *seeds* of the **sons of Terah**. The marriage and customary name pattern show Nahor had a wife named Micah and their grandson was named Aram; possibly the father of Milka proving kinsmen on both sides of the family. This Aram is the father or grandfather of Milka [Milcah], who was Levi's wife.

Ezekiel 16:1 notes, "Again the word of the LORD came unto me, saying, v2 Son of man, cause Jerusalem to know her abominations,

✦ THE EARTH ✦

v3 And say, Thus saith the Lord GOD unto Jerusalem; Thy birth and **thy nativity is of** the land of **Canaan**; thy father was an **Amorite**, and thy mother an **Hittite**." This proves Israel had intermixed with unbelievers and the Hittites are historical known as the descendants of Heth, son of Ham; who was the father of the Black race. Heth was the man that Abraham purchase burial land for Sarah and later he was buried there, because Heth was Abraham's distant relative. Ezra 9:1 notes, "Now when these things were done, the princes came to me, saying, The people of Israel, and the priests, and the Levites, have not separated themselves from the people of the lands, **doing according to their abominations**, even of the Canaanites, the Hittites, the Perizzites, the Jebusites, the Ammonites, the Moabites, the Egyptians, and the Amorites." All of the mentioned tribes or nations above were the descendants of Ham.

These verses were not talking about **Caucasians** mixing with Blacks, but people of color mixing with Blacks. The Hebrews were supposed to be "Yahweh believers", who were people of color. I'm not advocating all were Black, but Blacks were obviously in the mixing. Look at the color of those people that are currently living in these biblically mentioned areas with a heavy mixing of Caucasians genes for over two thousands years, they are still people of color. One of the sins these ancient people [Israel] was intermixing with "unbelievers", not the assumption given today "intermixing with another race was prohibited". God is all mankind Father, but **only** though "faith in Him." This is why God had to gave all mankind a new covenant [New Testament], because none of these ancient people were righteous, "**No not one**." Yahweh's **mercy** of overlooking their sins was asked for in their petitioned to Him to forgive them. Noah, Abraham, Job, King David and many more biblical righteous men committed sin. "I, even I, am He who **blots out** your transgressions, **for my own sake**, and **remembers** your sins **no more** Isaiah 43:25. That verse reveals the reason why these ancient men were called righteous. These men knew the Holy words of Yahweh and knew how to repent. Psalms 32.1 Thousands of years later Yahweh's mercy is recorded by the Apostle Paul in Romans 3:10. Paul stated, "I'm the **chief of sinners**" 1 Tim. 1:15. Man can't live up to Yahweh's Holy words, He must let those Holy words **live in Him**! God's Holy words will remind, correct, and strengthen anyone that will accept His written words. I'm thankful God is merciful and I hope you are too.

CHAPTER 16

Accepting your Calling

To everyone on earth, Yahweh has a calling on your life for a special purpose. Rather we accept His calling on our lives or we live for our own personal desires, it is our choice. Most of the time God will not force anyone to do anything. These are some of the men that accepted their calling, but most do not:

Samson was granted *supernatural strength* by God in order to combat his enemies and perform heroic feats such as wrestling a lion and slaying an entire army with only the jawbone of an ass. Two large gravestones of Samson and his father Manoah are located between the cities of Zorah and Eshtaol. Nearby stands Manoah's altar (*Judges 13:19-24*). Samson's activity takes place during a time when God was punishing the Israelites, by giving them "into the hand of the Philistines". The Angel of the Lord appears to Manoah, an Israelite from the tribe of Dan. Dan married Aphalcth, the **Moabite**. Now look at this biblical description of Samson; "**7 locks** of hair covering his **entire head**", meaning he wore **dreadlocks**. The truth can't be hid anymore. Read about your history and in this history is the living words of Yahweh. These Words are Spirit and they are life giving **John 6:63** These are not just stories, they are biblical truths. These words contains life, living, blessing, empowering and waiting though the years for you. "I knew you by name in your mother womb" Jeremiah 1:5. Can you believe it? If you believe the bible or you do not, it is the truth.

Just think, Yahweh is omniscient and He's omnipotent, and He knew each human being name before they were born. God does nothing unholy. "Well He's God", some may say. So let us look at these Godly men: Adam named all the animals that God created and he remembered them all by the name he gave them. Look at Moses, Joshua, Daniel, Elijah and Elisha miraculous faith in Yahweh. Notice Daniel, Ezekiel and the Apostle John; they were great revelators. Paul the Apostle, wrote more books in the New Testament than any other disciple. Finally, King Solomon was the wisest man on earth. How did they become such highly renowned individuals? They **asked** Yahweh and applied themselves to their petitions. What do you want to be for Yahweh? "Ask Him and it will be given." Matthew 21:22. This is not a metaphor, it is the truth, so apply your hands [finding yourselves doing them], your minds [studying Yahweh's WORDS and studying in schools], in the profession of your dreams with sincere devotion. This devotion should be as if you're seeking great riches or like you are staving and your favorite food is placed before you. Apply Godly desperate efforts to your petitions to Yahweh and you **will** receive anything you ask. As I've said before; Yahweh gives good things to those that love Him. Educate yourself; be diligent in your efforts to accomplish your dreams, thereby they will become reality. Yahweh says "I come in a book", so knowing this, your dreams and fulfillments are in books. Read them, everyone you can find and you will know trash when you read it. Your dream is locked in knowledge and knowledge come from books or divinely given by God to you and this spirit will drive you to more books.

Thereby, you will become knowledgeable, with this knowledge comes responsibility of helping the less fortunate. You thought you were receiving [God's] knowledge with no additional requirements? This book is written not only to motivate you; but to remind you, **"You are your brother's keeper"**. It is your choice to receive Yahweh's holy words. Test the spirits by your spirit 1 John 4:1. I'm trying to reveal to you the keys to Heaven, which requires you to produce Godly fruit [helping, informing and blessing others]. I'm not just trying to make you successful; if that is your only motivation in life, I suggest that you re-evaluate your goals.

I want to encourage many, regardless of race, sex or income status, so that I can produce some fruit that will be fit for the Kingdom. By doing this [encouraging others], when I stand before my Creator and His holy Angels open the Book of my life and then open the **other** Book, I can ask God for mercy; "Look how I've loved and shared your words" in which have no respect of person. I know that I need plenty of mercy, so I plead to you; help me with this cause by accepting and obeying the only living God. By helping me in this cause; you too can have all of Yahweh's righteous benefits for yourself. Afterward, you will produce fruit that is fit for righteousness. It is my hope that I've helped encouraged the next renowned person for Yahweh. *I believe if I shoot for the stars; I can only fall among the heavens*. Therefore, if I fail in my expectation of touching the next renowned person and I only help one single person; that one is enough. I would be satisfied and I would hope God will be satisfied in my effort.

You are so valuable to God; not only did His son die for your sins, but He also led me to pour out my heart to you. I've said some intimate things about my life in this book that I didn't care to say. God led me to share those intimate secrets. God told me; "Some of my people are hurt by this problem [shamed by the past]." Thereby, being led to do so, I've shared some things that most people do not reveal "Don't tell them your shortcomings." I haven't always been righteous and I confessed that fact. It's not something I'm proud of. I'm Yahweh's protocol son and must help you; "Be free of your pain", if you are in a spiritual state as I once was. If you are, as I was, I plead to you, "Come back home"! Our Father has a party waiting for you. Yahweh still can produce in you a spirit as he did in this man: Ezekiel, whose name's meaning: 'God will strengthen' (literally 'to fasten upon,' figuratively 'strong' and central protagonist of the Book of Ezekiel in the Hebrew Bible. Buzi was the father of Ezekiel the kohen (Jewish priest).

As I asked before about trusting Yahweh; what do skin color have to do with pleasing God? Nothing, so this book is written only to inform you of how good and merciful God really is and how all mankind evolved after the flood of the Earth. Since I've informed you of your ancestors history; now it is time to shoot for you dreams; because you now know who is behind you saying; **"This is my child and I will bless all that he or she touch. I will be in them. I will be favorable to them, and if, and when needed, I will chastise them, but I will always love them."** With this thought in mind, let's look again at the life of Rahab; this ex-harlot/whore became the bloodline of many important people. See how we are to look at life and with Yahweh's people? We can't condemn a person for anything, their race, their sins or any other reason, because God maybe is overlooking their sins or he will correct them.

Remember we are not in their prayer room or knows when they have repented. They might have repented, petitioned Yahweh, and the manifestation of their petition have not manifested itself in them when we look at their sinful acts. God is the only one that knows a man or woman heart. When man condemns another man personally, instead of only the sinful act, he have forgotten there is only one judge and we know him as Jesus. We have to forgive man offensives and overlook their sins, by praying for them and ourselves. We need to pray against all iniquity, we will receive as I've mention before "Yahweh's brownie points." This is our main christian job, "Love all mankind". "Love **covers a multitude of sins**" and I need plenty of covering [forgiveness]. 1 Peter 4:8. There is a biblical way to correct someone of sin Matthew 18:15-16. Notice, I didn't identify the one for his prideful act, "Calling a proclaim Jew anti-Semtic. Now look again at what happened in the past and what men did, including some of his descendants bathing in the pride of what they have done to with ancient history. Can you forgive them for what have happened in the past and present? Even if some says, "Those people are takers of unearned benefits and they are a bounce of takers." This is even said when the majority race are getting more of the social benefits than all the minorities together. I truly believe you can forgive, atleast this is my hope. Remember there are godly men in all races. You can't believe in man, you have to believe in your Father [God] and follower His holy words.

A few powerful men can't make a whole race evil or bad, that would be missing the point I'm trying to convey of Yahweh's "love". We as "Believers in God" have to trust Him and follow His spiritual guidance. As I look back on my life as a Soldier; mostly White men and women were the ones that have helped me the most and my own race did all they could to hinder me. One's blackness doesn't make him or her my brother or sister, it is their father that matters. So who are our brothers and sisters? The ones with the **same spiritual Father**. We, as a race shouldn't ask for a handout, but justice and fairness and sometimes a helping hand is needed. Regardless if they are lighter or whiter than I am, "Individuals that trust Yahweh, they are truly my kinsmen". The ones that don't trust Yahweh, I will treat with fairness and justice. I ask again what do our senses [looking like me] have to do with righteousness? If you interpret that this book was written to encourage hate against any race; that would be a incorrect assumption. Regardless of race, I will give honor and thanks to whoever it is due Romans 13:7. Remember this; we do not have a race issue as some attest too, but we have a love and hate issue. Will you learn to love righteously?

Heb. 3:7-8 says; "Today, if you hear his voice, **do not harden** your hearts as you did in the rebellion, during the time of testing in the wilderness, v9 where your ancestors tested and tried me, though for forty years they saw what I did. This was why Yahweh was angry with that generation; v10 reveal the truth, 'their hearts are always going astray and they have **not known** [receive] my ways. v11 So I declared on *oath* in my anger, 'They shall **never** enter my rest". This is what I want you to understand, Jesus didn't come to destroy the Law with its Commandments, "**He fulfill them.**" Mal.3:6 states "I the Lord do not change". I've heard many people say, "God doesn't do such horrific things". Thereby, showing they lacked spiritual teachings and understanding.

All of the adults from the whole Hebrew tribe that came out of Egypt except two [**Joshua and Caleb**] *"died in the wilderness"* and those two crossed over to the promise land with the offspring of our Hebrews ancestors [601,730 descendants over 20 years of age] Numbers 26:51. The 600,000 count (Exodus 12::37) were of men a foot [no women and children or the elderly were numbered] wondered in the wilderness for 40 years never to increase in numbers. God did this to know what was in their **hearts** Deuteronomy 8:2. The Cananites, Hittites, Amorites, Hivites and Jebusites [Some of Ham's disobedience descendants] lived in this land Exodus 13:5. Read Exodus, this wasn't the race of a people issue, it was a trust in Yahweh issue. This means that the Hebrews died in the wilderness because of disobedience; only because they **did not trust God** Hebrews 11:6. This literal "Promise Land" is a symbolic futuristic place of Heaven on Earth. This is our "Promise Land". Why only two of those adults made it? Read . . . *Numbers 1*, "They **trusted** Yahweh", instead of their *eyes*, "Let us go and conquer this land". There were giants in the land and the rest of the spies reported what their eyes saw, not believing in what Yahweh had told them, "I'll give you this land". Becaue of this unbelief; he humbled them Deuteronomy 8:2-17, v9:1-6, v10:22. Read those verses and know what is required of you. This make me think of what Apostle Paul stated in (Heb. 3) about the Old Testament prophecy for a generation after him. "That generation Paul is referring to is possibly this generation. "**I come like a thief in the night"** *(1 Thessalonians 5:2)*. Who is Yahweh talking to in these verses? I believe he was talking to everyone. Notice what David said in Psalms 32: "Blessed is he whom transgression is **forgiven**, whose sin is covered. (v2) For day and night they [my sins] were heavy upon me: My moisture [tears] is turned into the drought of summer." This means David didn't just say forgive me Lord, but he cried out for days to Yahweh for this forgiveness, "Create in me a steadfast spirit, I can't do it alone".

He truly repented before God. Let us learn from a man God calls, **"A man after my own heart"** and learn to humble ourselves before Yahweh. It's not like instant potatoes or coffee, it's like what Peter felt "I'm not worthy to die like my Lord". Crucify me another way! "Jesus, I continue in sorrow, even unto my death for what I've done to you", I can imagine this was Peter's thought. This is the life I live today; no man is worthy of God's grace, we just **except** His grace and put on His righteousness because He gives it freely. This is the biblical guided repentance. I've personally done so many bad things, I'm glad Yahweh has forgiven them all. Deuteronomy 9:7. Remember those things that were forgiven, don't forget! This why I write this book; I owe God so much and I want to love His people as He loves me. I'm not concerning myself with their ethnicity or who they are or what they have done. Yahweh is a forgiving God and will save anyone. As Peter once did, I once denied my God and I'm so thankful He has forgiven me. Yes, Preachers falls from grace too. I'm doing my best to show God that my heart will never grow cold again. So, I asked Him "Create in me a steadfast spirit" and this is the hope I live in; "waiting for the fullness of my petition to God to manifest in me."

Yet today, I'm still without full manifestation with all of my petitions, but God has empowered me with the gifts of Spirit that are listed in 1 Corinthians 12:3-12 and that reassure me I'm on the right track. My thoughts are always thankful, "Who is like God." I hope you will learn and receive those Gifts that operated in His disciples in the the Book of Acts in the Bible.

As with Peter, so I have this life reflection, "I'm so undeserving of his grace". But remember, we don't serve Yahweh with our **feelings**. We just trust Him in what he says, "You are forgiven, Holy, my child, anointed, my friend, I'll talk to friends face to face and I will empower you. Will you let him do the same for you? Just because we have been forgiven; I believe that we should never forget about those wrongful things we have done in the past. Do not be burden by them [no pity party], but being thankful for Yahweh's forgiveness and the goodness of Yahweh's grace in forgiving us of *all* the things we have done. Therefore I believe if we forget those past sins, we'll forget the fullness of Yahweh's goodness and mercy and I need plenty of mercy. Yahweh told us that *He* would forget our sins, but is there only one verse I've found in the Bible that we should forget our sins; *Philippians 3:13*. In this verse, Paul was not referring to forgetting his past sins in the literal sense, but only not to be burdened by them. If so, that would contradict him saying **"I'm the chief of sinners"** 1 Timothy 1:12-17. Many considered him a powerful saint and thought too much of him as he operated in God's Spiritual Gifts. He knew as well as any knowledgeable disciple Yahweh truths, **"I'm a zealous God"** and he was humbling himself. Paul was saying, "I reach for higher mark in Jesus/Yahushua and the *Key* to Heaven." Yahweh's word on a subject is establish in mouth of two or three and I find no other scriptural to prove this point as other ministers attest. Sometime we should bring these sins back up to Yahweh **only by** being more willing to forgive others, just to show Him how much we love Him for what He has done for us. This is why I'm sharing mine [past sins] with you, by showing you Yahweh's goodness toward me (I too, was once was the chief of sinners).

I know this sounds *strange* to some who read this, but read your bible and see the truth. This is not a hate message or boasting message, this is a love message. Some ministers say; "If Yahweh forgets our sins, then we should forget our past sins". Well, Yahweh's Angels are recording a book to open during Final Judgment. Those ministers may say, "Lord I thought you forgot; you told me you will." The bible also indicates that all our earthly deeds are written in a book. Rev. 20:12 states, "I saw the dead, small and great, stand before God and the book of life was opened, and **another book** was opened". When I face God; I'll ask, "Mercy O God, mercy on your servant" look at my mercy list [where I've loved and forgiven others] and multiply that list a hundred fold". **"The merciful will receive mercy"** Matthew 5:7. With that biblical quote, note the following verse: Mark 4:11 states, "Unto you [**the chosen**] it is given to know the mystery of the kingdom of God", but unto them

✦ THE EARTH ✦

that are without. (those that don't know; haven't treasured Yahweh's words as fine gold), all these things are spoken in **parables"**. The treasure of God's word teaches us his forgiveness and righteousness and is **worth its weight in gold**, more than precious pure gold.

The willingness of forgiving our brothers [all mankind] will give us the key to enter the City of Gold. I hope this sink into your spirit and guide you in all of your actions. So when someone wrongs you, mistreat you, hurts you without cause; you should know that you have been given a **golden opportunity**. Acts 5:40-41. Why not endure it, even rejoice in it and be glad? Can you see the way to the Kingdom now, so will you come? God is opening the door wide and he's waiting. Now, can you see what Jesus did for the thief on the cross, and how he too will be waiting to see you in heaven?

"I didn't have that knowledge; then you should excuse me", some may say when they see God during Judgement. There is a problem with that assumption; this knowledge is written to you. "Lo, I come in the volume of a book, **learn of me.**" I won't give you that verse, it up to you to find out your father's business, so you will be blessed and have *mercy* in the time of need. If you have read this entire book, you would have found that verse already. Meditate on its sayings; let it be the apple of your eye; nothing is more precious than the value of Yahweh's words.

If someone gave you 10 million dollars you would be so happy, excited and thankful. So here, I'm showing you the way to Eternal Life, where the City of Gold really is located. Value Yahweh's words, in them [words] lies life, health, riches and I mean unfathomable riches; in wealth, knowledge, power, mercy, love and whatever you can imagine in holiness. All of these things lie within Yahweh's WORDS. They will promote you, bring you honor, and people will marvel, "I knew that person, so what have gotten a hold on him or her." The City of Gold is not a metaphor, it really exists. If God said it and He did, then it's true. Revelation 21:18 God's word said it and He cannot lie. "Let it be said, let it be done", I know you heard those words before. Wise men will copy God's principles. Some men will make themselves righteous, thinking within themselves that you are not righteous, excluding all biblical principles to come to their righteous assumption. This is the way of the world, in which Yahweh told us to exclude ourselves." "If you belonged to the world, it would love you as its own. But, you **do not belong** to the world, but I have chosen you out of the world. This is why the world hates you". John 15:19. Even to the Hebrew tribe, Yahweh said; "Their hearts have gone astray" (2 Chronicles 6:37). I pled to you, then change your heart and come *back* to God/Elohim. If your relationship with God is not close, "Return your hearts back to God, which is our 1st Love." "What you ask the father in my name, he will give it to thee" (John 15:16). John 3:16, Romans 5:8, Galatians 2:20, Ephesians 2:4-5 and Psalm 86:15; within those verses Yahweh's love to man is sweeter than honey, its too good to be true, but it really is true, they are personal and direct, straight to you individually, as well directed to all mankind. Take them personally and then use them to love worldly men.

All of God's ministers are ordain to preach the truth even when it somewhat offensive. Ezekiel 33:8 states, "If you **doesn't speak** to warn the wicked from his way, that wicked man shall die in his iniquity; but his blood will I require at **thine hand.**" Considering that command, I plea to you to follow the principles of God. Regardless, if you are white, red, yellow, black or blue black, it doesn't matter, God loves you. So if God loves you [calling you His child], we ought to know what Mark 9:42 say about Yahweh's children.

"If anyone **causes** one of these little ones [those who believe in me] **to stumble**, it would be better for them if a large millstone was hung around their neck and they were thrown into the sea". These are our Father's statements and He says what He means. If I don't feel like loving someone, I'll ask our Father; "Create in me a new heart that **I will not sin against you**". "God loves everyone, so we have to love them too", this must be our thought and reasoning each and everyday. Our "feeling" have nothing to do with **believing** and **trusting** God. If we believe long enough in righteousness, our feelings will finally obey God too. Psalms 87:4 states, "I will make mention of Rahab and Babylon to them that know me". Why does

He make mention of a sinful woman and a sinful nation? Because God is a forgiver, He loves; He is merciful and full of grace. Who is like unto thee [God]? I've found no other god that does this! Man can tell good stories, but it is only one God that does this; "Loves his Enemies." So when you hear people talk about hurting others or harming them in any kind of way, they are being influenced by their spiritual Father [Lucifer]. "Well you said Yahweh will harden hearts" and yes I did, but He doesn't personally do it. He waits until Lucifer comes by, "Have you tired my Servant"? Job 1:6-9. Afterward, it's up to man to make the right choice (it is written in his Holy book how to **defend** ourselves), when Lucifer comes. "**Submit** yourselves, *then*, **to God**. Resist the devil and he will **flee** from you" James 4:7 Lucifer *tempted* Jesus, so you know he will tempt us. Jesus responded to him; it is written, it is written, and again, it is written; giving us a **lesson** on spiritual **warfare** Matthew 4:1-11.

"How can I love like God?" one might ask. "Be humble and love peoples that are not deserving of love as the world knows love and deal justly with all men", is Yahweh's directives. MICAH 6:8. Give honor to which honor is due, respect to whose respect is due and reverence to who it is due. It is not what church you attend or what doctrine they preach or faith they uphold, it just this simple, "LOVE". I will say it again, **"LOVE is the KEY"**. I can hear God say, "Look how my servant has **humbled** himself before me" 1 Kings 21:20-29. He said it about Ahab [descendant of Leah, wife of Abraham], who is mentioned in the bible as a wicked man. Yahweh called him, "Servant". Ahab had humbled himself and Yahweh forgave him, but Yahweh knew Ahab's heart would harden again. Think about what God thinks of you; if you do these things. Remember, men love to hate and judge, but God's truth is "Love", and true love has no boundaries, with the same measure we have sown, we will reap in due season. May God bless you and keep you in His presence. May you be blessed in all things that whatever you put your hands too, and may it manifest, multiply and bare forth fruit that is fit for God's purpose. Remember in Micah 6:6 Yahweh showed us what is good and what He requires of us, "Do justly, **Love mercy** and *walk humbly* before God". These acts will cover all sins.

The reason color is not as important as one with pride might think, God appearance is all of the colors on earth. Ezekiel 1:27, "And I saw as the color of amber and the appearance of fire v28 as the appearance of the **bow** [rainbow] that is in the cloud in the day of rain and I fell to my face." Thereby, we need to fall on our face before God!

BIOGRAPHY

James L Taylor Sr. is the son of Henry Taylor; whose great-grandfather was a former slave. He was born on a Mississippi Plantation in 1958. He is a product of the Orange County Public school system in Winter Garden, Florida. He attended Valencia C.C in Orlando, Florida in 1976; afterward he retired from the US Army in 1997. He was self-educated in the history of warfare, Spiritual Discipline Meditation as a soldier. He was an astute student of Theological and Spiritual Doctrine. He has the biblical Spiritual Gifts of the Spirit of Knowledge, Wisdom, and of Faith.

Taylor accepted Christ at an early age and surrendered to preach at age 21. He served as Assistant Pastor of Holy Light Deliverance Church of Columbus, Ga.

He is married to Loretha Taylor. To this union two children have been born: Tweetie and James Jr.

SELECTED BIBLIOGRAPHY AND REFERENCES

(BEYOND ROOTS "In search of Blacks in the Bible), William Dwight Mckissic, Sr)

(Babylonian Talmud Sanhedrin 70a)

David Noel Freedman, Allen C. Myers, Astrid B. Beck, *Eerdmans dictionary of the Bible*, (Wm. B. Eerdmans Publishing: 2000)

Rogers, J.A 100 AMZING FACTS ABOUT THE NEGRO WITH COMPLETE PROOF. Helgo M. Rogers, 1970 edition.

(The Persian historian Muhammad ibn Jarir al-Tabari (c. 915)

A Short History of the World by H.G. Wells, New York: MacMillan, 1922.

Josephus (Antiquities of the Jews I.6).

The German historian Johannes Aventinus (fl. c. 1525)

(PreHistoric Nations by John D. Baldwin, New York: Harper & Brothers, 1869, John W. Marshall, New Delhi: Asian Educational Services, 1996,

(A Study in Hindu Social Polity by Chandra Chakaberty, Delhi: Mittal Publications, 1987)

(Signs & Symbols of Primordial Man by Albert Churchward, Brooklyn:A&B Books Publishers, 1993.

From Babylon to Timbuktu by Rudolph R. Windsor. Atlanta: Windsor's Golden Series, 2203

(It Began in Babel by Herbert Wendt. New York: Delta Dell Publishing Company, 1964)

(From Babylon to Timbuktu by Rudolph R. Windsor. Atlanta: Windsor's Golden Series, 2203, (A Study in Hindu Social Polity by Chandra Chakaberty, Delhi: Mittal Publications, 1987.

Bryant, T. A. TODAY'S DICTIONARY OF THE BIBLE, Minneaplois, Minn. Bethany House Publishers, 1982.

Burns, Edward Mchall. WORLD CIVIZATIONS. NewYork, N.Y.: W. W. Norton and Company, 1982.

Du Bois, W.E.B. THE NEGRO. New York, N.Y.: Oxford Unversity ©

David Livingston ANCIENT DAYS 203-2012

(Compton's Interactive encyclopedia first published in 1922)

(PreHistoric Nations by John D. Baldwin, New York: Harper & Brothers, 1869.

Gaston Wiet, etc, "The Great Medieval Civilizations: cultural and scientific development. Volume 3. The great medieval civilizations. Part 1", Published by Allen and Unwin, 1975.

(It Began in Babel by Herbert Wendt. New York: Delta Dell Publishing Company, 1964, pg. 368.)

History of Ethiopia, Vol. I., Preface, by Sir E. A. Wallis Budge.)

(Herodotus an ancient Greek historian)

Gordon Wenham Themelios 11.1 (September 1985): 15-18.],

Patrick T. English, Cushites—Cush, son of Ham, Colchians, and Khazars, Journal of Near Eastern Studies, vol 18, Jaunuary—October 1959, p. 53.]

African Origins of the Major Western Religions," 1970, p. 76).by Dr. Yosef A. A. Ben-Jochannan, an Ethiopian Jew.

Anthropologist, Count Constatin de Volney (1727-1820)

(George Syncellus, the *Book of Sothis)*

(Nigerian Boundary of the Jebu-Sheba Confederation) written by Alice C. Linsley.

Dr Patrick Darling, an archaeologist (Nigerian Boundary of the Jebu-Sheba Confederation). *(*The 1892 New York Times report*)* (Pseudo-Philo's account (ca. 70)

Saint John of Damascus, Theologian (c. 645 or 676-4 December 749)

The Compton's Interactive encyclopedia.

(Conflict of Adam and Eve with Satan) by Dennis Hawkins, framents of *Cave of Treasures*

(Gunther Plaut, The Torah: a Modern Commentary, 881. New York: UAHC, 1981.)

Count Constatin de Volney (1727-1820 Anthropologist Egyptian findings Report)

(AotJ Book 1:6/2). Pliny the Elder Nat. Hist. 5.1 and Ptolemy Geog. iv.1.3)

(Introduction to the Study of African Classical Civilizations by Runoko Rashidi, London: Karnak House, 1992, pg. 69).

(Wilhelm Gesenius' Hebrew grammar; The **Lexicon Manuale** was subsequently translated to English in America by Edward Robinson D.D. in 1836) (The British scholar and theologian Tregelles published his own version in 1846, which was reissued in 1857 with special warnings in a section "To The Student" about scholarly attacks on Christianity and the dangers of Gesenius' rationalism).

Friedrich Müller in his Grundriss der Sprachwissenschaft (Wien 1876-88).

In Search Of "Ancient Israel" (London and New York: T. & T. Clark Publishers, Ltd. 1992) ISBN 0-567-08099-4.

Cities of the Biblical World: Qumran (Cambridge: Lutterworth, 1982)

F. Leo Oppenheim—Ancient Mesopotamia

Georges Roux—Ancient Ir

✢ The Earth ✢

Franz Rosenthal, trans., *The History of al-Ṭabarī* (State University of New York Press, 1989), Volume 1, pp. 10-11

Tubb, Johnathan N. (1998) "Canaanites" (British Museum People of the Past) p.15

"Bloodline of the Holy Grail" Laurence Gardner

THE ORIGIN OF MAN

God's Creation of Color

Brief Overview

This history of mankind has revealed he has produced great inventions, wonderful works of art, discoveries, and has created a fragile family unit. The Love of man has been revealed in our souls by; poetry, history and by his devotion to his God. Man's efforts of love have slowly declined over his years on Earth. It needs to be motivated and patiently encouraged. This is my intent for writing this book; that one might grow in their love and touch the world that starving for godly love. Godly love is not like man's love; it has no expectations, no paybacks; but given freely without cause. I hope to motivate this godly love within you.

God created the world and made it a world of many colors. He beautified the world the colors of the rainbow. Everything that God created was colored to His perfection; including man. Man does not see the things created by God as perfect as they were created, because man only visualize with his eyes. God expected man to visualize the beauty that He created with all of His senses; including His spiritual sense; His heart.

Marketing
Keynote or elevated pitch:
-God created the world; and made it of many colors. He beautified the Earth with the colors of the Rainbow. These colors are in all living things, including Man.
Key search words
Origin of Man, Man of many Colors, or The Love of Man.
Primary readers; all
Category:
Religious-Motivational

INDEX

A

Aaron 31, 32, 52, 53, 83, 105, 106, 108

Abinadab 107

Abraham 16, 18, 19, 20, 21, 22, 23, 34, 35, 37, 38, 39, 40, 41, 42, 43, 44, 47, 48, 49, 51, 61, 75, 87, 103, 111, 112, 113, 114, 115, 127

Abraham And Nahor 21, 113

Abraham's Ancestors 21, 39

Abraham's Brother 113

Abraham's Father 21, 44, 114

Abraham's Mother 114

Abraham's Sister 114

Abraham's Wife 38, 39

Abram 22, 23, 48, 76, 103

Absalom 55, 104, 108

Adam 13, 20, 21, 28, 88, 118, 134

Aethiopia 25

Africa 17, 25, 27, 28, 29, 34, 35, 36, 38, 47, 60, 61, 65, 73, 74

Agape 82, 85, 98

Ahab 127

Ahaz 108, 109

Ahimaaz 107, 108

Ahitophel 55

America 50, 59, 60, 62, 69, 70, 71, 73, 110, 134

Americans 68, 69, 73, 76

Ammihud 104

Amos 33, 74, 109

Amram 53, 105, 106

Ancestors 17, 21, 38, 39, 47, 52, 55, 58, 59, 65, 68, 73, 74, 83, 94, 112, 113, 120, 121, 122

Anti-Semitic 65, 72

Apostles 92

Arabia 20, 21, 25, 35, 39, 41, 55, 61

Aram 17, 23, 105, 111, 113, 114
Aribath 48
Ark 13, 14, 24
Armoni 107
Arpachshad 16, 18, 34
Arphaxad 15, 16, 29, 40, 44
Asenath 110
Ashbea 46, 53
Asher 48, 49, 73
Asia 15, 17, 25, 27, 28, 29, 30, 35, 36, 41, 64
Assyria 18, 33, 41
Azariah 103, 104, 109

B

Babylon 26, 29, 30, 33, 34, 56, 64, 126
Babylonia 26, 29, 30
Bashan 108
Bathsheba 54, 55, 59
Beerah 47
Ben 65, 105
Benjamin 48, 106, 111
Bethuel 43, 113, 114
Biblical Doctrine 9, 66, 104
Biblical Ethnicity 101
Biblical Forefathers 28
Biblical Land 20, 28, 29
Biblical Scholars 15, 19, 53
Biblical Times 63, 71, 105
Biological Father 51
Bithiah 103, 104

Black Gene Lineage 54
Black Genes 46, 54, 107, 108, 109
Black Heads 17, 28, 111
Black Race 22, 23, 26, 31, 39, 48, 49, 61, 64, 70, 105, 115
Blacks 20, 27, 30, 34, 41, 42, 50, 51, 58, 59, 61, 64, 69, 70, 71, 72, 82, 103, 112, 115
Black-Skinned Descendant 63
Black Slavery 59, 70
Blind 44
Bloodline 52, 55, 103, 120, 135
Blood Sacrifices 31, 101
Boaz 46, 51, 52, 54, 111
Book Of Genesis 15, 16, 17, 21, 24, 32, 33, 37, 43, 110
Book Of Jubilees 15, 16, 17, 19, 22, 34, 38, 49, 105, 114
Books Of Samuel 106, 109
Budge, E. A. Wallis 35
Buz 56, 112, 113

C

Cainan 16, 18
Caleb 102, 103, 122
Calneh 23, 26, 33
Canaan 14, 18, 23, 24, 25, 26, 27, 28, 38, 43, 48, 49, 55, 59, 67, 103, 110, 111, 112, 115
Canaanites 18, 22, 25, 27, 28, 38, 42, 48, 51,

53, 57, 61, 104, 111,
112, 113, 115
Chaldeans 19, 21, 23,
31, 34, 35, 111
Chaldees 16, 21, 22,
34, 111, 113
Chedorlaomer 23, 37
Chononicles 52
Chozeba 46
Chronicles 13, 17, 18, 25, 26,
46, 51, 53, 54, 102, 103,
104, 107, 108, 110, 126
Churchward, Albert 31, 132
City Of Gold 77, 125
Colchians 64, 133
Color 9, 10, 28, 42, 47, 50,
51, 53, 55, 56, 58, 59,
60, 63, 65, 71, 74, 75,
77, 81, 86, 103, 106,
110, 115, 120, 128, 137
Commandments 42, 59, 67,
69, 70, 96, 121
Concubine 107, 110, 114
Covenant 14, 32, 37, 38,
83, 98, 103, 115
Cush 19, 21, 23, 24, 25,
26, 29, 34, 38, 39,
42, 56, 61, 109

D

Daniel 118
David 38, 50, 51, 52, 53,
54, 55, 59, 85, 88
Dedan 26, 56, 61
Descendants Of Judah 52

Descendants Of Shem 22, 28
Deuteronomy 59, 66, 68, 69,
70, 74, 122, 123
Disciples 87, 92, 93,
96, 98, 123
Doctor 57
Doctrine 9, 32, 66, 98, 104, 127

E

Earthly Genes 50
Eber 16, 18, 19, 21, 34, 38,
41, 45, 48, 52, 55,
61, 103, 106, 113
Egypt 18, 21, 24, 25, 26,
31, 35, 38, 39, 41, 42,
47, 49, 52, 56, 59, 60,
61, 62, 63, 64, 67, 68,
70, 73, 104, 105, 106,
110, 111, 112, 122
Egyptians 18, 24, 26, 31,
39, 60, 62, 63, 64,
67, 69, 71, 104, 106,
110, 112, 115
Elam 15, 17, 40
Eliam 55
Eliezer 43
Elishama 104
Enslavement 59, 73, 74
Ephraim 65, 102, 104, 109, 110
Er 53
Erech 21, 26, 32
Esau 43, 44, 45, 109, 112, 113
Eshtemoa 53, 103, 104
Ethiopia 20, 25, 27, 33, 34,
35, 41, 56, 67, 71

Ethiopians 34, 35, 47, 65
Ethnicity 19, 22, 28, 42, 46, 47
Ethnicity Black 50
Euphrates River 17, 21, 22, 23, 29, 30, 33, 47, 111
Eve 134
Exile 47
Exodus 31, 52, 62, 63, 67, 70, 104, 105, 108, 112, 122
Ezekiel 13, 33, 94, 105, 108, 114, 118, 119, 120, 126, 128
Ezra 110
Ezra 104, 105, 115

F

Faith 115, 118, 127, 129
Fasting 94
Five Sons Of Shem 16, 17
Forefathers 28
Forgiveness 69, 82, 85, 88, 120, 122, 123, 125
Founder 26, 29, 53, 105, 111
Founding Father 37
Fruit 57, 62, 71, 77, 119, 127
Fullness 123, 124

G

Gederah 53
Genes 28, 46, 107, 109, 110, 114, 115
Gershon 105, 106
Gershonites 104, 105

Gesenius 48, 134
Gilboa, Mount 106, 107
Gilead 47, 106, 108, 111
God 10, 13, 14, 21, 23, 24, 28, 31, 38, 42, 45, 49, 51, 52, 57, 58, 59, 60, 62, 66, 67, 68, 70, 72, 75, 76, 77, 81, 82, 83, 84, 85, 86, 87, 88, 89, 90, 91, 92, 93, 94, 95, 96, 97, 98, 100, 102, 103, 104, 110, 111, 113, 115, 116, 117, 118, 119, 120, 121, 122, 123, 124, 125, 126, 127, 128
Godliness 57, 70, 72, 84, 93
Gospel 9, 13, 16, 50, 51, 87, 112

H

Hadurah 48
Ham 13, 14, 19, 21, 22, 23, 24, 25, 26, 27, 35, 36, 38, 41, 45, 49, 64, 70, 108
Hamito-Semitic 17
Ham's Descendants 14, 23, 28, 55, 56
Haran 22, 113, 114
Heaven 31, 32, 66, 71, 72, 74, 75, 93, 98, 101, 119, 122, 124, 125
Heber 18, 42, 103
Hebrew Ancestors 68
Hebrew Bible 15, 16, 22, 34, 43, 50, 104, 120

Hebrew Bible/Old Testament 50
Hebrew Descendants 81
Hebrews 13, 32, 35, 38, 49, 52, 58, 59, 62, 64, 69, 81, 86, 87, 88, 89, 113, 115, 122
Hebrew Scholars/Priests 75
Hebrew Shene 34
Hebrew Tribes 46, 65, 112
Hebron 44, 53
Herodotus 25, 35, 64, 71
Heth 115
Hittites 17, 27, 57, 104, 115, 122
Holocausts 59, 73
Holy Spirit 9, 54, 93, 94, 95, 98, 99
Horite 114
Horite Priests 114
House Of Ashbea 46

I

India 20, 28, 30, 35, 60, 74
Intermixing 22, 27, 35, 47, 49, 55, 57, 65, 112, 115
Isaac 40, 43, 44, 45, 113, 114
Isaiah 13, 31, 33, 57, 67, 88, 109, 115
Israel 21, 28, 42, 46, 48, 57, 64, 72, 74, 75, 102, 103, 104, 105, 106, 107, 110, 114, 115
Israelites 9, 18, 25, 27, 37, 39, 43, 47, 51, 53, 63, 67, 104, 106, 108, 111, 117

Israelite Tribes 111

J

Jacob 43, 44, 45, 46, 47, 48, 49, 51, 70, 75, 103, 105, 106, 110, 113, 114
Japheth 13, 15, 16, 24, 41
Jasher 40, 45, 46, 48, 49, 114
Jasher, Book Of 40
Jebu 39, 40
Jebu-Sheba Confederation 133
Jebusites 27, 38, 39, 57, 104, 115, 122
Jehallelel 103, 104
Jeremiah 35, 42, 47, 56, 58, 69, 76, 84, 109, 111, 113, 118
Jerusalem 28, 38, 39, 42, 47, 55, 64, 93, 108, 114, 115
Jesus 9, 32, 50, 51, 52, 54, 57, 58, 60, 69, 72, 75, 76, 77, 83, 86, 87, 88, 91, 92, 93, 94, 95, 96, 98, 100, 110, 112, 120, 121, 123, 124, 125, 127
Jesus Lineage 46
Joash 46, 53
Job 19, 20, 36, 48, 56, 87, 111, 112, 127
Jobab 19, 49
Jochebed 105, 106
Joel 47, 104, 109
John 30, 57, 60, 66, 75, 85, 87, 88, 95, 96, 97, 98, 100, 112, 117, 118, 119, 126

Jokim 46, 53

Joktan 19, 20, 21, 38, 39, 40, 41, 42, 49, 52, 55, 56, 61, 114

Jonathan 27, 105, 107, 109, 110, 113, 114

Joseph 51, 54, 62, 63, 65, 67, 70, 77, 102, 108, 110, 111

Josephus 15, 17, 26, 30, 64

Joshua 21, 28, 42, 52, 53, 100, 102, 103, 104, 105, 110, 118, 122

Jubilees 16, 17

Judah 28, 40, 45, 46, 47, 51, 52, 53, 55, 101, 102, 103, 104, 109, 111

K

Kasdim 34, 35

Kenizzites 103

Kesed 16, 22, 34, 35

Ketu 39

Ketu-Jebu 39

Keturah 19, 38, 39, 40, 41, 48, 49, 61, 112

Khawm 64

King Nimrod 19, 21, 23, 26, 29, 32, 34, 56

Kohath 53, 105

L

Laadah 46, 53

Laban 44, 45, 49, 113

Lamentation 56, 58

Land Of Ham 24, 25, 64

Land Of Shinar 23, 29, 32, 33

Law 31, 70, 83, 96, 121

Leah 45, 47, 49, 105, 127

Lecah 46, 53

Levi 28, 52, 53, 62, 105, 106, 110, 111

Levites 53, 104, 105, 115

Libya 26

Lord 9, 21, 28, 31, 32, 41, 48, 58, 66, 67, 68, 73, 74, 75, 77, 82, 83, 84, 85, 86, 87, 88, 89, 97, 98, 103, 114, 115, 117, 121, 122, 123, 124

Love 28, 37, 51, 57, 58, 60, 66, 67, 70, 72, 75, 76, 81, 82, 84, 85, 87, 89, 90, 96, 97, 98, 100, 107, 118, 120, 121, 123, 124, 125, 126, 127, 137

Lucifer 31, 60, 74, 86, 127

Luke 13, 16, 17, 18, 22, 42, 51, 52, 75

M

Machir 108, 109, 110, 111

Madai 15, 16

Malachi 67, 105, 110

Malchishua 107

Manasseh 108, 110, 111

Mareshah 46, 53

Mark 75, 91, 92, 124, 126

Marriage 34, 36, 40, 43, 49, 52, 54, 55, 57, 107, 113, 114

Mary 54, 63

Masoretic Text 18, 22
Matthew 13, 42, 50, 51, 52, 57, 59, 60, 66, 82, 83, 85, 86, 95, 118, 120, 124, 127
Medad 105
Menes 26
Mephibosheth 107
Merab 107, 108
Merari 105
Merarites 104, 105
Mered 63, 103, 104
Mesopotamia 21, 22, 23, 29, 30, 32, 33, 38, 43, 44, 56, 113
Micah 75, 84, 107, 109, 111, 114, 127
Michal 95, 107, 108
Midian 41, 47, 48
Milcah 22, 106, 112, 113
Miriam 53, 63, 103, 105, 106
Mizraim 24, 25, 26, 49
Moab 52, 53, 54
Moabites 27, 50, 51, 52, 53
Moses 14, 31, 41, 42, 52, 53, 62, 63, 83, 84, 96, 103, 104, 105, 106, 108, 118

N

Naamah 55, 112
Nago-Jebu 39
Nahor 21, 22, 112, 113, 114
Nahshon 51, 52, 111
Nathan 52, 54, 55

Nazareth 52, 87, 91
Nebo 47
Nehemiah 47, 109
Netaim 53
Nigeria 39
Noah 13, 14, 15, 16, 22, 24, 25, 27, 36, 39, 47, 59, 115
Noah's Son 14
Nuba 47

O

Obedience 72
Old Testament 24, 35, 50, 51, 65, 101, 110, 111, 122

P

Padan-Aram 113
Patriarchs 13, 14, 43, 49, 52
Paul 87, 93, 116, 118, 122, 124
Peleg 19, 21, 38, 39, 40, 48, 52, 55, 106, 114
Perez 40, 46, 102, 109, 111
Peter 13, 82, 84, 94, 96, 101, 120, 123
Pharaoh 26, 31, 62, 63, 67, 71, 103, 110
Philistines 26, 44, 53, 56, 106, 111, 112, 117
Phineas 108
Phoutes 26
Phut 24, 26, 108
Prayer 85, 94, 120

Pride 56, 57, 60, 61, 65, 66, 71, 72, 73, 86, 93, 98, 120, 128
Progenitors 17, 18
Promised Land 25, 52
Prophet 105, 106, 108, 109, 110, 113
Prophet Samuel 105, 106
Proudness 74, 95
Psalm 25, 31, 64, 84, 85, 91, 92, 93, 95, 97, 100, 115, 122, 126

R

Raamah 25, 38, 55, 56
Rahab 51, 52, 102, 111, 120, 126
Ramesses 67
Ramses 67
Rebekah 43, 44, 113
Rebellion 64, 71, 121
Rechabites 42
Red Sea 19, 20, 41, 52
Rehab 51, 52
Reu 21
Reuben 46
Reward 67, 75
Righteousness 87, 88, 100, 119, 121, 123, 125, 126
Romans 28, 60, 71, 77, 116, 121, 126
Rotheus 49
Ruth 46, 50, 51, 54

S

Sabaeans 19, 20, 55
Sala 18
Salathiel 54
Salmon 51, 52, 54, 111
Samson 117
Samuel 50, 53, 54, 55, 84, 104, 107, 108
Sanctification 87
Sarah 39, 43, 103, 111, 114, 115
Saraph 46, 53
Saul 48, 106, 107
Semitic 13, 15, 17, 18, 28, 34, 35, 39, 41, 52, 55
Septuagint 16, 18, 22, 30, 42
Serpent 39
Serug 21, 22
Seti 63
Sheba 19, 20, 25, 38, 39, 41, 42
Shelah 18, 45, 46, 52, 53, 54
Shem 13, 15, 16, 17, 18, 22, 24, 25, 27, 28, 29, 34, 35, 36, 38, 40, 41, 44, 45, 49, 103, 113
Shinar 20, 22, 23, 26, 29, 32, 33, 34
Shobal 102
Shuah 41, 45, 46, 54
Sidon 27, 61
Simeon 28, 42, 45, 47, 106
Sinites 27
Sinners 74, 88, 116, 124

Skin 20, 42, 47, 48, 50, 55, 56, 58, 59, 65, 86, 120
Slavery 50, 59, 60, 67, 68, 69, 70, 71, 73, 77, 81
Slave Trade 65, 68, 73
Solomon 20, 42, 51, 54, 55, 108, 111, 113, 118
Son Of Judah 46, 52, 53
Spies 52, 102, 122
Spiritual Father 121, 127
Spiritual Food 83, 91, 93
Strabo 35, 56
Sumer 29
Sumerians 23, 29, 30, 31, 34

T

Tabernacle 52, 64, 105
Tamar 40, 45, 46, 52, 54, 111
Targum Jonathan 110, 113, 114
Terah 21, 22, 23, 44, 103, 105, 113, 114
The Land Of 16, 17, 19, 21, 23, 24, 25, 26, 28, 32, 41, 47, 48, 52, 56, 61, 64, 69, 103, 111, 115
Torah 49, 105, 108, 113
Tower Of Babel 18, 20, 56
Tribe Of Ephraim 102, 104, 109
Tribe Of Judah 28, 46, 47, 52, 53, 55, 102, 103, 109, 111
Tribes 27, 28, 30, 35, 36, 46, 50, 65, 73, 106, 111, 112, 115

True 28, 30, 31, 42, 54, 57, 58, 59, 61, 65, 66
Trust 60, 70, 77, 86, 89, 121, 122, 123
Truth 9, 10, 28, 32, 42, 58, 59, 72, 75, 76, 77, 84, 85, 89, 92, 98, 103, 104, 112, 117, 126, 127
Turkey 15, 23, 32, 33, 60

U

Unbelief 88, 91, 122
Ungodliness 57, 59, 70, 75
Upper Nile 25, 30
Ur 16, 21, 22, 23, 34, 113
Ur Kasdim 34
Uz 56, 112
Uzziah 109

V

Volney, Constatin De 71

W

Wells, H. G., 30
Wendt, Herbert 30, 31
Wisdom 42, 48, 58, 91, 92, 93, 98, 104
Word Of Yahweh 77
Words (Living Words) 97, 101, 117
Words (Spiritual Words) 84, 94